# OHIO's
### *greatest* GOVERNOR

To Armonde,

Po was the Best Dad, Grandfather and Great Grandfather. He loved his family.

Love you
Mama Sue
2013 Pop Pop

# OHIO'S

*greatest* GOVERNOR

# James A. Rhodes:
*Politician of the Century*

*by* BYRL R. SHOEMAKER

*Shoemaker Enterprises*
Columbus, Ohio

Additional copies of *Ohio's Greatest Governor: James A. Rhodes:
politician of the century* may be ordered directly from:

Shoemaker Enterprises
92 Ceramic Drive
Columbus, OH 43214

Library of Congress Control Number: 2005905803

*Photographs courtesy the Rhodes family and the
James A. Rhodes State College*

Dedicated to the competent and hard working

men and women who served on Governor Rhodes' staff

during his four terms in office

# Table of contents

# Foreword

About two years before he died, Governor Rhodes asked me to write his biography. Over the next two years I would go to his home and sit with him and try keep him telling me about his life in some orderly fashion. That was almost an impossible task. He was so interested in all that was going on in the world that he would go from past to present constantly. Also, he was concerned that he not demean or embarrass any person. Many times he would say, "You can't put this in the book but let me tell you...."

I would take notes and get his story of his life on tape and then attempt to translate it into somewhat of a continuous record of his life. Also, he made available to me the several books that had been published covering parts of his life as he was honored by both Republicans and Democrats long after he had left office.

I have known James A. Rhodes since he became governor for the first time and knew of him since he was elected the mayor of Columbus, the youngest ever mayor of any major city in the nation. I worked closely with him in the development and expansion of technical education and the great expansion of vocational education.

He increased funding for higher education and all areas of education more than any other leader in the century. Education, however, was only one of the areas touched and greatly changed and improved by this man of vision. Many people are aware of the area of their life that he touched but few know the whole story of the many contributions that he made to the lives of the people of Ohio.

It was a privilege to work with but not for with the governor over the sixteen years that he served the people of Ohio honestly and well. I had a great respect for him when I started his biography and even a greater respect when I finished. He selected able and hard working people to work with him and gave them leadership, respect and opportunity to serve the people. First for the city of Columbus and then the state of Ohio. He liked people and was just as comfortable and interested in talking to the custodian of the building as he was the president of the United States, and had a respect for both of them.

This biography is not only a report of the life of a great man but also of the accomplishments of the great men and women that worked with him for the betterment of the citizens of Ohio.

—*Byrl R, Shoemaker, Ph.D.*

*greatest* GOVERNOR

An intentful 4th grader in Jackson, Ohio (first row, third from right), James Rhodes had seemingly learned at a young age to avoid party factionalism.

# Hard times

"But Mother, the paper bag drags the ground when I walk," Jimmy complained as he looked at the newspaper bag his mother brought to him.

"That's all right," his mother replied. "I'll shorten it by stitching up the shoulder strap and it will be off the ground."

"Mother, all the other kids are older than me," Jimmy said, continuing his objections to the new responsibility. "I'm just 9 years old."

"It's all right, son," his mother continued. "They all started when they were 9 years old."

Jimmy gave several examples of young men older than he, but each time his mother answered, "Yes, but they all started at 9 years old."

That was the end of the discussion and Jimmy, at the tender age of 9 years, found himself with a paper route and forty customers.

The day before, they had buried his father. The Rhodes family was living in Indiana where Mr. Rhodes was the superintendent of a coal mine. It was 1918, the time of the great influenza epidemic, and Jimmy's father died in a Jasonville schoolhouse where many of the victims had been taken because there were not enough hospitals to care for the massive numbers.

There were no pensions available to coal miners, and the Rhodes family had gone quickly from relative prosperity to poverty. The family returned to bury the father in Jackson, Ohio, where there was a family plot and where Mr. and Mrs. Rhodes had lived for a number of years before going to Indiana when Jimmy was seven years old.

The family now occupied a different status. "We were on the giving end before, and then we were on the receiving end," Jimmy would recall as an adult.

James Rhodes was born in Coalton, Ohio. The family home before his birth was in Jackson, where his Welsh ancestors had arrived from the coal mines of Wales, settling in the coal mining section of Ohio. Since it was the custom for the family to return to their original house for the birth of a child, the parents rented a house in Coalton for Jimmy's birth on September 13, 1909. He was christened James Allen Rhodes, and soon after, his family moved back to Jackson, Ohio.

Jimmy's grandfather owned a coal mine, and Jimmy's father worked with him until he became superintendent of the Indiana mine. During the years before the death of his father, James A. had been part of a loving family. Welsh people were known for being honest and hard working and required discipline from their children.

Jimmy remembered later that his father was a 'Republican for a cause.' He explained: "It came from John

Lewis of the Mine Workers. My father belonged to the United Mine Workers before he was on the managerial side of the coal mine. Lewis was fighting for free schoolbooks and Lewis was a Republican. So my folks followed him. They were Republicans for a cause."

He also remembered a time around Halloween when boys gathered a bunch of green tomatoes, and waited near a "Chic Sale"—the euphemism for an outhouse (named after a humorist who wrote a widely read book on how to build a privy). The boys then threw the green tomatoes through the crescent or star, which provided an opening in the door on the front of the backhouse.

As Jimmy prepared to throw what must have been his tenth tomato, he was suddenly lifted off his feet by a hard kick from the rear. As he landed and turned, there was his father. All the way home, his father boosted him occasionally from the rear. That was the end of his experiences in peppering backhouses with green tomatoes.

*D*uring the two years he lived in Jasonville, Indiana, which was about twenty-five miles south of Terre Haute, he lost a brother and a sister and finally his father. His father died in November of 1918, and Jimmy remembered well the first Christmas after his father's death.

On Christmas Eve, Mother Rhodes called the three children together. Between them, she divided an orange, an apple, a banana, and a sack of peanuts that had been given to them by a neighbor of friend. "Children," she said, "there is no Santa Claus. You are only going to get what you work for."

There were no tears; it was merely a fact of life. The

next morning they went to church, and that was their Christmas celebration the year Jimmy's father died.

Since there were no pensions then for coal miners, the children and the mother had to go to work. Jimmy picked up junk, such as iron, walking the alleys, then selling what he had found. He caddied, cut grass, cycled, ran errands, delivered groceries, picked berries, helped move families—anything to make a nickel. He worked for a few hours a week in a small confectionery, for a dollar.

He fished, hunted, caught water moccasins, trapped muskrats for forty cents a pelt and sold crawdads, twelve for a nickel. He would say later that his early youth was excellent, and that he he had everything there was in the way of a boyhood.

There was a baseball diamond near their home, so he sold pop at the games. Then he got a regular job. Due to the increase in the number of students in the school, the school board had to bring in portable classrooms. Jimmy was given ten dollars a month to keep the portable building clean. He served as janitor: Big money!

When the school board added another portable building, he was able to get a janitor's job for his sister. He didn't tell his sister the job paid ten dollars a month. He cashed both checks, gave her nine dollars, and kept the other dollar for himself.

He figured he had a good thing going until his mother found out about it. At that point, he received a lesson in honesty. She forced him to give back to his sister every dollar he had withheld from her money.

The Cochran family was one of the well-to-do families in Jackson, and Jimmy worked for them for a short time. He first drove an automobile at the age of ten, delivering chickens for the Cochran family.

"I probably had the most enlightening boyhood of any boy," he said in an interview. "I had a mother who believed in discipline and obedience. My mother had one thing she taught us all. It was to pray every morning and every night, and the prayer was this: 'Oh God, help me be somebody.' That was her whole theme, that anybody can be what they want to be if they work at it."

"I had to work and I knew it, and it made me stand apart in any group. I was probably the only one making any money in the crowd, and helping to support a family. I gave my mother every cent I earned. I was always looking for a job, something to do, someway to make money. I always had a great respect for older people. I was taught that. I think from your parents comes the path you are going to follow."

The Rhodes family had been Methodists and his mother sang in the church choir. Jimmy did not like to dress up for church, so she told him to sit on the curb outside the church, where he could hear her singing.

Like many young boys, sports became a part of his life and a group of boys would gather in a field near the Presbyterian Church to play ball. The pastor of the Presbyterian Church finally came out and asked, "Do you young people like to play ball here?"

"Yes!" they answered.

"If you want to play here," the pastor told them, "you will have to join and attend our church."

Jimmy and the other boys joined the church and attended the catechism classes, and they continued to play ball in the churchyard.

Jimmy hustled for jobs and money and he learned to work with adults.

*I*t was an extremely difficult time for the Rhodes family. Mother Rhodes worked two jobs, four or five hours at the cigar factory, and another four or five hours at the shoe factory. A number of people were kind to the Rhodes family, dropping off a watermelon or some other food. Occasionally, relatives from another city dropped off used clothing, but most of the clothes were not wearable and Mother Rhodes threw them out. There were no welfare or child support funds in that time.

Still, Mother Rhodes was fiercely independent. The county commissioners came calling one day, knowing the difficult time that faced the family. They told Mother Rhodes they were there to take the three children to the county orphans' home, where would be cared for until they were old enough to help take care of the family.

Mother Rhodes' broom immediately went into action and with it, she drove the three county commissioners up the street. They didn't even stop to take their automobile. There would be no orphanage for the Rhodes children.

The family was part of that large group that could have put on the front of their house the motto, "Poor but honest and hard-working." Yes, the place in which they lived had been a chicken coop and in the winter they often had to go to bed to keep warm, but there was no time for moaning about their hard luck. There were slop jars at night, the Chic Sales was out back, and the poverty was physical not moral, spiritual, or mental.

When Jimmy was 13 years old, the family moved to Springfield, Ohio. Jimmy Rhodes started to high school in that city. Mother Rhodes went to work in a restaurant to support the family and young James began to make his mark in athletics.

During his first summer in Springfield, his athletic

ability made him a part of the American Legion baseball team. That American Legion Team won the district championship, the state championship, and the national championship. When school started in the fall he was playing ball with the American Legion team, and he didn't bother to start school until the season ended.

He went out for the football team and started practicing. The principal called him in and told him he was suspended for not attending the first period of the school year. The principal informed the coach to drop him from the team. Jimmy, however, had started to play quarterback and the coach was so impressed with his ability that he made a plea to the principal to reinstate him. On the basis of the coach's appeal, Jimmy was allowed to return to school.

At one of the games, a linemen from the opposing team came through and hit Jimmy hard in the stomach and knocked the wind out of him. As he lay on his back, Mother Rhodes came out of the stands and began beating the referee on the head with her umbrella. They finally got Mother Rhodes back into the stands and the game continued. Jimmy played on the football, baseball, and basketball teams while in high school and graduated from Springfield High.

An early entrepreneur, Jimmy began to book bands when he was only 15. When he did this, he insisted that Mother Rhodes stop working. At age 16, he had his own dance hall, The Greystone, receiving assistance from the man that had the Greystone dance halls in Columbus and Dayton.

Jimmy worked hard, was friendly to all people, and

the adults wanted to help him. Thus the Springfield years were wonderful years. He grew in his athletic skills and became an entrepreneur. For the first time since the death of her husband, Mother Rhodes did not need to work to keep the family together. And at the age of 16, Jimmy Rhodes became the family breadwinner

Working five jobs and playing varsity basketball, young Jim increasingly learned a variety of skills including selling, promotion, booking bands, newspapering, and business management. He had no particular desire to go to college, but he graduated with a basketball scholarship. He earned four letters in high school, for basketball and football. A yearbook writer called him a "good fast guard" in basketball, and he also played tennis.

"Everybody in school liked him," said Charles Fox, the retired principal of Springfield High. "He was a good school citizen. He was a promoter. Even then he always had something in the fire."

The difference between a young man who became the only four-term governor of Ohio and a possible juvenile delinquent was a wonderful mother. When James A. ran for mayor of Columbus, Ohio, someone asked him who was his campaign manager.

"My mother is my campaign manager," he said.

"What does she know about politics? She can't be your campaign manager."

"She knows right from wrong and that's all she needs to know," Rhodes said.

Mother Rhodes did not preach, but she was not backward in giving guidance to her children. Basic concepts she taught her children were honesty and work hard. This simple creed would serve as the basis for the political life of James A. Rhodes.

When Mother Rhodes was left destitute with three children to rear, not only did she go to work to support the family, she insisted that the other members of the family work to help with their own support. She believed there was no excuse for begging or whining. The fact that a paper bag made welts on Jimmy's back was no excuse to not continue to carry the papers and contribute to the needs of the family. And when Jimmy did something of which she did not approve, he would feel the whack of her broom.

When the family lived in Springfield, Jimmy became popular with the girls. When the girls rang him up, Mother Rhodes would not bring him to the phone. She sat him down one day and told him bluntly that he could get into more trouble with illicit sex than he could by robbing ten mail trains.

During his political life, Mother Rhodes often listened to his speeches.

"You're on the right track," is all she would say in commendation.

He achieved his goal of having his mother stop working when he was about age 15 when he started to book bands in Springfield, and he saw that she was well taken care of for the rest of her life.

When he started booking bands, he would go into the kitchen where she was getting dinner and stand quietly counting his money over and over until she would notice him and ask, "What do you have there?"

Then he would finally take off some of the bills and hand them to her. She would protest but grab the bills, put them in her bosom, and tell him to never give her money again. The next week he would do the same thing.

Mother Rhodes was equally strict with the sisters.

When they became adults, Jimmy continued to be concerned with their welfare. Both of the sisters went into training to be nurses. One of them was told to gather the false teeth of the patients and to wash them. She gathered the teeth and put them in a tub and washed all the teeth at one time. It was both tragic and hilarious when they tried to identify the teeth for the people after they were washed together in the tub.

Mother Rhodes lived her creed and insisted that James A. and his sisters also live by that creed: "Be honest and work hard; you don't win it, you earn it."

# HARD TIMES
*Chapter one*

# Sidewalk university

The cheers of the crowd urging the two basketball teams to victory filled the old Coliseum at the Ohio State Fair ground. The Dayton Stivers and the Springfield High Schools were locked in a close game to determine the state championship for 1927. The leading score bounced back and forth between the two evenly matched teams. It had been a long road to the finals and each of the two teams was sure of victory. As the final buzzer sounded there was a great roar from the supporters of Dayton Stivers.

Jimmy Rhodes had played hard but his Springfield team lost as Dayton Stivers made the winning basket in the last seconds of the game. Jimmy was disappointed but the game was over.

As long as he had done his best, he was satisfied, and it was time to go on to the next chapter in his life. He never took the time to worry over what might have been; he spent his energy on the next challenge.

The coach of Dayton Stivers High was the legendary Floyd Stahl, who was selected after the championship

James A. and Helen with Grandmother Rhodes, and daughters Susan (left) and Saundra. Garnet, the nanny, is behind Susan.

season to be the coach of the varsity basketball team at The Ohio State University.

As coach Stahl took over the reins of the OSU basketball team, he remembered the Springfield player that had given his Dayton Stivers team a hard time. He contacted Jimmy Rhodes and offered him a scholarship. An OSU basketball scholarship did not pay much in those days—$25 a quarter. This was not nearly enough to support a player who also was the sole support of his mother and two sisters.

Jimmy Rhodes, however, had been booking bands for fraternities and sororities at OSU during his senior year in high school. He had been working with three bands led by Michael Hauer, Jack Walkup, and Harold Weishmeir. Michael Hauer urged Jimmy to move to Columbus to enhance his band-booking business. Jimmy accepted the scholarship offered by Coach Floyd Stahl in 1928, and soon he was practicing basketball and promoting his band-booking business.

When Jimmy Rhodes came to Columbus, he became known as "Dusty" Rhodes, a likely nickname that related to his family name. He was already the main booking agent for three bands. As he moved to Columbus, he began to expand his business to book larger nationally-known bands.

Although Floyd Stahl had recruited Dusty Rhodes to play basketball at OSU, his time as a basketball player was very short. He started to practice with the freshman team and Coach Stahl knew that players on scholarships needed additional funding and he arranged jobs for them. He came to Dusty at the end of a practice and told him that he had arranged a job for him waiting tables at the Phi Gam house during the noon hour.

Dusty was making money booking bands and he told Floyd Stahl that he was pledged to that fraternity and probably was the only pledge that had been able to pay the initial dues. Dusty handed the basketball to Coach Stahl and said, "If you ever find me with a basketball in my hands again, you have the right to hit me along side the head with a 2 by 4." Except for community teams, that was the end of Jimmy Rhodes' basketball career.

As he finished his first semester that spring, cancer struck Susan Howe Rhodes. He summarized his dilemma as follows: "I had to make a choice. This was my mother, and this was my family. It costs a lot of money to fight cancer, and there wasn't any Medicare or Social Security then. I made up my mind that education was status, but this was my mother, and I was going to take care of her.

*Chapter two*

She had taken care of me. The education I was getting was not meaningful in my evaluation. I am not anti-education, but it didn't mean that much then. It would help me in status, but it couldn't help my mother."

So Rhodes expanded his line of operations, and became known around campus as one of the few persons with money in his pocket. Living near campus, he began attending classes without paying tuition. He would go from class to class, especially law classes, and sit in. In 1932, through the influence of his mother, Rhodes became interested in politics. He became president of The Ohio State University Republican Club and organized a campus committee for Clarence Brown for Governor.

During his years as governor, James A. and several other well-known persons who attended but did not graduate were awarded Varsity O letters. This group included such people as Jack Nicklaus and Jesse Owens, and they were given recognition for their accomplishments and community services.

The academic career of Dusty Rhodes at The Ohio State University was short-lived. He had started to work at the age of 9 years, and became the major support of the family at age 15. He out-hustled the young people of his age and became a major booking agent for bands in Columbus. He was totally committed to the practical world and had no patience with education that did not seem to have a relationship to work and success. As he entered his studies at OSU, he was required to take a course in Spanish. Studying Spanish did not make any sense to him. He asked the professor, "Where can I use

Spanish anywhere within 1,500 miles of Columbus?" The professor told him that he needed so many courses of Spanish to graduate from college. He dropped Spanish. Other courses included in his curriculum did not make sense to this young man who was totally committed to making a success of his business. He was booking major bands and had made many friends with student groups and faculty members at OSU and influential people in the Columbus area. He never met a stranger, and he had always worked well with adults. After two quarters at the University, he left the academic world.

Dusty set up an office in the basement under Smithy's Drug Store, where he worked with his band-booking business. During this period of time, he booked about fifty percent of the bands used at the University functions. The future Governor also began to book bands—Benny Goodman, Lionel Hampton, Cab Calloway, Les Brown, and Gene Krupa—into the Olentangy Park Gardens. The Olentangy Amusement Park was in its heyday and a major attraction for the people of Columbus and the surrounding area. The Heinlins owned the Park and became friends with Dusty Rhodes. They used his services to book big bands into the Olentangy Dance Gardens.

The Heinlins challenged Dusty to bring Guy Lombardo to the Olentangy Gardens. Guy Lombardo was the top band in the nation, and Dusty was able to get Guy Lombardo for an October date. The Heinlins were elated. He also booked bands into Valley Dale, the other mecca for dance enthusiasts in the Columbus area.

For those who do not remember the Depression, wages at that time were strictly make-do: construction workers, $907; typists, $625; waitresses, $525; steelworkers, $424; store clerks, $370. The best paying job was United States

Congressman—$8,670 a year. Prices were equally low: plate lunch, 35 cents; hot dog, 5 cents; oatmeal (one pound box), 5 cents; a man's wool suit, $10.50; haircut, 20 cents; and a new Pontiac coupe, $585.

It was during this period that Dusty Rhodes started the Si U Fraternity. The Sigma Epsilon Fraternity was one of the most prestigious in the nation but did not have a chapter at OSU. Dusty got the idea of forming a fraternity for persons who hung around Smitty's Drug Store and he named it Si U, a take off on Sigma Epsilon but standing for Side Walk University. Persons could belong who had attended—but not necessarily graduated from—OSU. The dues were only two dollars and a large number of young men became members of Si U.

*D*usty Rhodes was initiator of the fraternity and guiding hand, but he did not serve as president of the organization. Many athletes became members of Si U. Membership included such persons as Sid Gillman, Woody Hayes, Jumping Joe Williams, Bill Carroll, Lou Hinchman, and many of the athletic greats of OSU. The groups gathered at Smitty's Drug Store—located at Sixteenth and High Streets—and Bob's Tailor Shop, which was next door.

The fraternity held a banquet once a year on the campus. The fraternity was initiated in 1936, and even after Rhodes was governor of Ohio members would call asking when they would have another meeting.

During Dusty Rhodes' band-booking period, he was making money, as well as making friends. He also received honorariums from the Music Corporation of America. He was accorded the honorary title of "Mayor of University City." He would remain friends with many of the greats in the music and entertainment world, including Benny Goodman and Lionel Hampton, who would call him on his birthday.

At the time, it was difficult for even a well-known black person to be accepted into a first class hotel. Dusty Rhodes would have them as guests at his home. He also became friends with Bob Hope and for many years played in the Bob Hope Golf Classic. He attended in California the last big birthday party held for Bob Hope, some years after he had served his last term as governor and the first time that he had purchased and worn his own formal tuxedo.

Five years after Dusty Rhodes left the academic classes at OSU, he opened a restaurant and named it "Jim's Place." It became one of the gathering spots for athletes in the University area. Grant Ward helped him to establish the restaurant, and Dusty ran the restaurant for about four years.

Understanding the Depression and the intense competition for jobs to keep family together and a little money in one's pockets is to understand Jim Rhodes, who made "Jobs and Progress" his theme throughout life. His own experiences proved to him that a job was absolutely essential to human dignity and satisfaction. The choice of giving up a college diploma in order to earn was an obvious one to him—and thousands of others who began their lives in the great Depression. It was also obvious that politics offered a career—as well as the on-the-job training—for the Depression generation.

During this period of his life, the future governor did not become wealthy in terms of money, even though he was able to maintain himself, his mother, and his sisters in reasonable comfort. He did, however, became wealthy in terms of friends, in business experience, and in contacts with influential people who pointed him toward a life in politics.

# 1
# Politics 101

Lee Remlinger, a colorful character, had a barbershop at 16th Street and High, and James Rhodes had his band-booking office in the basement underneath. Athletes and prominent people came to Remlinger's barbershop for his services. One day a man named Chick Coleman came in and Lee asked him how he wanted his hair cut. "In silence," Chick Coleman told him.

Grant P. Ward visited the barbershop every day for a shave. He was a prominent politician, serving as a state senator, an attorney, and had gained public recognition as the announcer of Ohio State football games. Senator Ward was a member of Varsity O and through his position in the senate, his political connections, and his relationships with The Ohio State University, he was an influential person in both state and local politics.

The young man with a lot of hustle, James A. Rhodes, became acquainted with Grant Ward, and they became friends. Ward was impressed with this brash, hardworking, personable young man, and he

~Dapper James Rhodes (at right) on High
Street in 1936 during his fraternity days.

encouraged Rhodes to run for committeeman of the 16th
Republican ward, the largest Republican ward in the city
of Columbus.

In 1938, with Grant Ward's support and guidance,
James A. was elected ward committeeman and retained
that position until he was elected auditor of the city of
Columbus about eight years later. In his position as ward
chairman he came into contact with the political forces
of the Republican Party.

Under the guidance and sponsorship of Grant P.
Ward, James A. was elected journal clerk of the Ohio
House of Representatives. The office of the journal clerk
was responsible for reporting what had happened in the
house of representatives and to identify the activities
that were projected for consideration. Rhodes served as

the journal clerk for about five years but continued his lucrative activities in booking bands. During this period of his life, Rhodes was making both money and friends. His election as ward committeeman and journal clerk of the house of representatives gave him an introduction to Politics 101.

*E*arly in 1938, the members of the city board of education came to a rather serious disagreement. The contentious issues within the board gained the attention of the news media and the citizens of Columbus. The men who gathered at the barbershop joked with James A. about running for the Columbus School Board, a non-paying position. When Grant Ward joined with the others to encourage his candidacy, James A. accepted the challenge and ran. It was his first time in a public election.

With the mentorship of Grant Ward, Rhodes ran for the city board of education and was elected. His usual hustling style, self-confidence, and candid approach to campaigning won over the voters in spite of his young age, and Rhodes became an active member of the board.

About six months into his first term on the board, Branch Rickey called James A. and asked to meet with him. Rickey owned the St. Louis Cardinals and had purchased the AAA baseball team in Columbus and named it "the Red Birds." Rickey was interested in promoting the "Knot Hole Gang" membership for the youth in Columbus. Members of the Knot Hole Gang had to be under a certain age, and as members they could attend the Red Bird baseball games free. The concept was that adults would accompany the youth and swell the attendance of paying customers. Only about 600 tickets had been distributed in the initial effort.

Branch Rickey asked James A. to use his position on the board of education to promote membership in the Knot Hole Gang through the schools. Rhodes always had an interest in sports and youth and readily agreed. He approached the superintendent about having the teachers, at an appropriate time, take a few minutes and sell the tickets to the youth for ten cents apiece. Even at that time, Rhodes did not believe that people valued any thing they received free.

The head of the Columbus Teachers Association came to Rhodes and pointed out, in no uncertain terms, that teachers were not going to be the means to sell the tickets to the young people. No one would profit from the sale of the tickets. Any money received from the ten cents per ticket would be given to the City Recreation Division, and the youth would get into the baseball games free. In his usual way, Rhodes didn't argue; he bided his time.

About six months later, a proposal for a teacher's raise came before the board of education. As the board met to consider the proposed salary increase, Rhodes asked the superintendent and the other board members if he could take the proposal home to study it. With approval by both the board and the superintendent, he took it home and somehow it was misplaced. No action was taken on the proposal for several months.

The head of the Columbus Teachers Association came to see Rhodes and asked when consideration would be given to the proposal for a teacher's salary increase.

Rhodes explained that might happen after the teachers decided to sell the Knot Hole Gang tickets.

The representative of the Columbus Teachers Association explained to Rhodes, in unkind terms, the teachers were not going to sell Knot Hole Gang tickets. Again, Rhodes did not argue the issue but the proposal for the teachers' increase did not return to the board of education for consideration.

After a few months passed, the teacher representative asked Rhodes when the teacher increase would be considered.

"When the teachers sell the Knot Hole Gang passes," he answered.

The leadership of the teachers reconsidered their position and sold the passes. The school board then passed the proposal for the teacher's increase.

Obviously the teachers did not mind selling the passes, since it took very little time and provided the youth with an opportunity to attend baseball games free. A total of 30,000 tickets were sold to the youth and the $3,000 was given to the city recreation department. Columbus now had the largest Knot Hole Gang in the nation.

Young people came to the games in droves and filled part of the field around the scoreboard. Branch Rickey asked Rhodes to trim the number of youth in the Knot Hole Gang but he refused. He pointed out that such an action would cause a backlash that would hurt the Columbus franchise. Instead, he proposed they divide the members into groups and indicate the days they could attend. It worked.

The Columbus Red Birds ended the year with the largest paid attendance figures of any team in the league. Everyone gained, including the teachers, youth, and the

Columbus baseball franchise. This became the basis for the political decisions that James A. Rhodes made during his long career in public office: Don't argue, bide your time, and attempt to make winners out of all parties in a dispute.

Branch Rickey was elated. The management of all the baseball teams in the AAA league asked Rhodes to accept a position to promote the Knot Hole Gang program across the nation. James A. refused the offer and remained in Columbus.

During the time James A. served on the Columbus School Board, he continued to book bands and to work as journal clerk in the house of representatives. Also, he began a courtship with Helen Rawlins. Helen was a beautiful girl and soon became his steady girlfriend. On the basis of his many activities, his hustle, and his growing public acceptance, James A. was selected by the Junior Chamber of Commerce as the most eligible bachelor in Columbus.

As Rhodes was walking along the street with Helen, a pretty girl came up and gave him a big kiss, right in front of Helen. As she left Helen was furious and tuned to him and said "I got a good look at that girl, and if I ever find you with her after we are married, I will shoot you first and her second." There was to be no sharing of affections with other women after the two were married.

Grant Ward liked Helen and went to New York to buy a wedding ring for James A. to give to Helen. On his return, Grant was heading to the Capitol Building, the ring in his pocket, when he dropped dead near the statue of President McKinley. James A. did not accept the ring for his marriage to Helen, since he believed it belonged to the family of Grant.

*D*uring Rhodes' second term on the school board, the city auditor, Walter Otto, went to jail for illegal activities in office. Since the Democrats were in control of city council, Blaine Holloway was appointed interim auditor, and an election was required to fill the position. Persons were elected for city offices on a non-partisan ballot, but the Republicans and Democrats supported persons for each of the offices.

At the time of the election for the new auditor, four people were on the ticket—Blaine Holloway, the interim auditor; Mr. Coyle, the father of the band leader Ziggy Coyle; Robert Otto, who had been let out of jail and wanted his job back; and James A. Rhodes.

In 1939, the Republican Party endorsed Rhode's candidacy. Walter Otto, however, remained on the ticket. At this time Rhodes was still the committeeman of the 16th ward. He campaigned on a platform to clean up the mess and the theme that "2+2=4 not 5," referring to the problems that that brought about the downfall of the previous auditor, Walter Otto.

James A. was elected, and his political career was underway. He was elected to two terms as city auditor, but he served only one and a half terms because he decided to run for mayor.

Rhodes proved to be an outstanding auditor. The *Columbus Dispatch* of June 30, 1943, wrote: "He had worked to put the city on a 'pay as you go' plan of operation, began paying employees by check instead of cash, and initiated and carried out the overhaul of the city's bookkeeping system."

James A.'s interest in athletics and youth became an important part of his public service and remained a part of his interest and efforts throughout his public life. These efforts were not politically motivated, but they did help to build a political base for the future. One of the many civic activities begun by Rhodes was the Central Ohio Men's Service Fund, an organization that raised funds to buy athletic equipment for service men in central Ohio. James A. served as president of the state AAU, and commissioner of the Ohio AAU. He gave leadership to the central Ohio boys' and girls' basketball tournaments from 1940–1942, he organized and directed a central Ohio junior cage tournament for girls and boys between the ages of 9 and 18, and he found time to supervise the AAU wrestling and swimming events for four years.

James A. always had a passion for golf and he was good at it. Always concerned about the little people, he noted there was scant attention paid to the caddies. As president of the Ohio Public Links Association, he organized the National Caddie Tournament Association and provided the first tournaments for the caddies. He also found time to establish the All-American Newsboys Sports Scholarships.

All these activities served to expand his political base, but the expansion was not his goal. James A. Rhodes was always interested in the welfare of people, especially youth. He was just as interested in—and comfortable— talking with a homeless person as he was with the President of the United States. To Rhodes, however, there were never any small people. He had a true passion to help to improve the lives of people that he served, and he was honest, simple, direct, and innovative.

*A*s auditor, James A. did not have police authority, but he learned about the city's finances, and the malfeasance of government that allowed gambling and prostitution to flourish in Columbus. Columbus had one of the worst crime rates in the nation. Even though Mayor Green had campaigned on the platform "Get out of the Red with Green," the city was in bad shape, both socially and economically. Numbers running was rampant in the city, gambling was prevalent, and prostitution flourished.

All efforts by civic organizations and the churches to reduce crime in Columbus had been ignored by the city administration. As auditor, Rhodes observed these problems, but he had no power to solve them. In 1943—because of inept city management and the control of Columbus by the criminal element—he decided to run for mayor.

Since the city had a non-partisan ballot, the candidates for mayor included incumbent Mayor Green, county sheriff Jake Sandusky, Rhodes, and two others.

Mayor Green wanted to debate Rhodes and a date was set. Green started the debate with his slogan, "Get out of the Red with Green," and spoke about the greatness of his achievements. Rhodes told about the payoffs made to the Green administration by the gamblers and the land given to Green by gambling interests.

As Rhodes told what he had learned as auditor of the city, Green ran out the back door, and the *Dispatch* reporters had to chase him to get an interview.

After the primary, the election was between Jake Sandusky and Rhodes, and a time was set for another debate. Rhodes went to a 14th ward meeting in the United Commercial Travelers Building and said he intended to announce at the debate Jake Sandusky's illegal relationship to the Columbus crime element. Sandusky had six deputies sitting in the 14th ward meeting. They reported back to Jake Sandusky and said, "This man is crazy."

Rhodes went from the meeting at the 14th ward to the sixth floor of the K of C Hall on State Street where the debate was to take place. Sandusky was on the first floor but wouldn't come up to the room for the debate.

"Jake," said Rhodes, calling from upstairs, "come on up and take your medicine."

Sandusky didn't show, and on November 2, 1943, Rhodes was elected mayor of Columbus, the youngest mayor of a major American city.

Before the election, Preston Wolf invited Rhodes to the *Dispatch* offices and took him in to meet H.P. Wolf, the man in charge of all the Wolf activities and enterprises.

"What are you going to do about the most prominent gambler in the city of Columbus?" H. P. Wolf asked Rhodes.

The gambler named by Wolf had the center of his operation in the neighborhood of Fifth and High Streets and seemed thus far to be above the law.

"I will throw his ass in jail," Rhodes said.

"You can't do that," H.P. said. "No one has been able to touch him."

"I am going to be sworn in at 3 p.m. today," Rhodes said, "You call me at 3:15."

Wolf called Rhodes at 3:15 and asked, "What did you do with that gambler?"

"His ass is in the county workhouse along with the other rats," Rhodes said.

$\mathcal{J}$his action by the new mayor illustrated another principle learned from his mother: "If you make a promise, keep it."

As the new mayor, Rhodes was going down one of the divided flights of stairs in the Neil House, and associates of the gambler were going up the other stairs. They used all kinds of nasty language to demean the new mayor. Columbus had an ordinance against such, and Rhodes had them arrested.

The little boy who started to carry papers at age 9 and become his family's major bread winner was growing in stature—with both friend and foe.

# The youngest mayor

James A. Rhodes was overwhelmingly elected mayor of Columbus on November 2, 1943. James A. received 40,799 of the 70,217 votes cast, for a 58 percent majority over his opponent, Jacob Sandusky. Six weeks before, Rhodes had turned 34 years old, making him the youngest mayor in the history of Columbus—and the youngest mayor of any major city in the nation.

He had campaigned to clean up Columbus. He had attacked both Sandusky and Green, his opponents, as being responsible for the Columbus "open city." A report from one of his campaign speeches, in the *Columbus Dispatch*, September 10, 1943, read:

> The question to be answered by the voters of Columbus on September 27 (primary date), is whether Columbus is to

James A. in 1941 when first
elected mayor. He was 32 years old.

*be cleaned up or remain as it is today. The billboard twins*
*(i.e. Green and Sandusky) are teaming up—you see the big*
*glossy billboards. If this is a challenge to good government,*
*I accept it and hurl it back to the racketeers and gamblers.*
*They are out to beat James Rhodes. They are after me and*
*nobody else. They want to nominate the other two men and*
*play it safe.*

Rhodes inherited a mess: Gambling, numbers, prostitution, loan sharking, and street crimes. The city was in financial trouble. Instead of paying down its bonded debt, the city had simply refinanced it. The general fund was in the red by $832,229 and there was $1,387,000 worth of back pay claims of city employees, money withheld from the employees during the Depression.

An article in the *Ohio State Journal* said:

> *(The city) literally turned the municipal court into*
> *a collection agency to collect great numbers of fines from*
> *gambling and vice rackets. Gambling operators were*
> *permitted to post large sums of money with the municipal*
> *court for 'fines.'*
> *Rosters of gamblers' employers were provided. Each day,*
> *clerical aides wrote dozens of 'arrest' sheets from the rosters,*
> *and fines were automatically deducted from the deposits.*
> *Police were not required to pick up gambling violators,*
> *nor were those 'arrested' even required to appear in court.*
> *The fines were periodically transferred into the city's general*
> *fund for routine operating purposes.*
> *Then the city government turned to 'traffic enforcement'*
> *to increase revenues. Police were given weekly quotas of*
> *arrests to make for traffic violations....*
> *The succeeding period —1939 to 1943— put the*
> *finishing touches to what little public confidence was left*
> *in the city government. Not only was confidence in the*
> *competence of the government destroyed, but confidence in*
> *its very integrity came to an abrupt end....*

Rhode's first official action was to move Mike DeAngelo, a major gambling king in the Columbus area, from his silk-sheeted bed in a local hospital to the city workhouse. DeAngelo had been convicted of having several number winners attacked and thrown from his building into the middle of High street. He had been permitted to stay in a hospital bed and was playing cards with several of the policemen, supposedly guarding him, when he was unceremoniously moved to the Columbus Workhouse, at the order of the new mayor.

Said the new mayor: "I inherited a city inhabited by good people and saddled by bad government."

One of Rhodes' first actions was to establish a policy that if a person was caught with a numbers slip in their possession, he would be judged as guilty as the person who had written the slip and serve the same sentence. The penalty for writing or for purchasing a numbers slip was set at thirty days in jail and a $1,000 fine.

The numbers racket was based on selling chances to people. The purchaser would guess at numbers taken from the stock market report for the day on which the number was purchased. The payoff was on the basis of five hundred to one, thus a bet of five cents on a number would return $25 to the bettor, and many people became addicted to this form of gambling.

The policy of making the purchaser as liable for prosecution as the seller worked. Almost overnight, the numbers racket stopped in Columbus and moved to the county, where numbers players received the same lenient treatment as they formerly received in the city. Since the population of the county was not as large as the city, however, the numbers racket ceased to be a major problem in the Franklin County area.

The garbage collection pattern, which had been sporadic, was put on a regular basis. Piles of trash and mountains of ashes had collected in the alleys of Columbus because there had been no plan or service of collection. During Rhodes's first term, collection of rubbish was re-established. Rats had taken over sections of the city and a rat extermination program was initiated by Rhodes, and the city was cleaned up.

Columbus had become famous nationally for the large potholes in the city streets which damaged cars daily. Rhodes initiated a street repair plan. Police and fire protection services were increased and improved. He established a "Write the Mayor week," to encourage citizens to identify their concerns and interests.

A Democratic committeewoman from the south side of the city complained that every week cars were damaged by a monstrous pothole in front of her house. Rhodes went to visit her and she said, "I'm a Democrat and you came to see me?"

"You wrote me a letter and I am here," he said. Then he saw that the pothole was repaired.

The committeewoman called Walter Heer, the head of the Democratic Party in Columbus, and told him that from then on, "I am backing Rhodes."

Rhodes tried to beautify city hall by planting tulips, but due to the lack of funds the number of tulips was small. The government of Holland heard about his efforts, and about the small number of tulips he had available, and sent him 10,000 tulips free of charge. Rhodes planted them around city hall and invited the citizens of Columbus to come to City Hall to see the beautiful display, not just to pay fines and register complaints.

Rhodes continued his work with youth in cooperation with the new recreation commission, voted in at the same time he was elected mayor. The common touch and a sincere interest in youth have been illustrated in many ways. To report one illustration: Rhodes learned that young people were ice skating on the Olentangy River near the football stadium, and he sent city workers to clean the ice and set up floodlights so the people could skate safely and enjoyably. He also asked for and received a gift of some ice skates from Smith's Skating Rink—even though the Smith Rink was for roller skates—so that those that lacked money for skates could participate.

*F*or many years, the Hoover brothers, who were in charge of the water department, lobbied for a dam to increase the amount of water available to the citizens of Columbus, and the water shortage had become critical. Rhodes put a bond issue on the ballot to build a dam, his strong promotional effort encouraged the people to pass the bond issue, and a dam was placed on Alum Creek, north of Columbus. This new dam relieved the water shortage and provided for the growth of the city.

Because of the dedication of the two Hoover brothers operating the water department, the dam was named and dedicated by Rhodes as The Hoover Dam.

Rhodes knew that a job was essential for the welfare of the individual and that people with jobs made for a prosperous city, state, and nation, and so "Jobs and Progress" became his rallying point. As mayor he brought in the Westinghouse Corporation, General Motors, and the American Trotting Association.

During his first term, his administration levied a three percent tax on utility bills to repair city streets. He increased sewer charges to the suburbs and raised license fees to taxicabs. These resources brought the city out of the red for two years. In his second term, however, a decision by the Ohio Supreme Court found the utility tax unconstitutional and the tax was repealed in 1946.

In order to maintain the fiscal integrity of the city on a pay-as-you-go basis, a five percent income tax was proposed by Rhodes and enacted by a vote of the people.

This tax pulled the city out of the red and placed it on a sound financial footing. The first year of the tax brought in over $2 million dollars and paid all the past due bills. Two years later, the yield was up to $3.5 million. The benefits of this tax included a million dollars worth of police, fire, and garbage equipment; the hiring of additional policeman and fireman; regular garbage collections; and an expanded recreation program.

The young mayor was fearless, and if necessary he could also be ruthless in support of programs he thought were essential for the welfare of the people that he served. His approach during his service to Columbus was the same that he followed for the rest of his public life: "What do you need? Let's get it."

When it came time for re-election, he was opposed by Green, who ran as a Republican and Dailey, a Democrat. At the time of the election, a *Columbus Citizen* editorial read:

*We believe the best interest of Columbus will be served by the re-election of Mayor Rhodes. He may not be the ideal mayor but he has worked faithfully in the interest of the city and demonstrated a desire to give it good government.*

*The administration of Mayor Rhodes has been clean and above board. The open and widespread gambling that flourished in some former administration has been notably absent from his regime.*

*On the other hand, he has helped promote clean entertainment and has cooperated in things which make Columbus a better city.*

*Columbus is at a point in its history where it needs to improve its standards as a metropolis. The services of recreation, health, safety, planning, and transportation*

Mayor Rhodes (at right) riding with President Truman (back seat, left) and Governor Lausche, circa 1950.

*all need improvement. During the Rhodes administration progress has been made on all of these, but much remains to be done.*

*Mayor Rhodes has made a good record in spite of severe financial limitations. We believe he will continue if his fellow citizens re-elect him, to bring to his job as chief city administrator the spirit of progress and cooperation which is necessary for the growth and improvement of this metropolis.*

He won the second term handily, and the city council became one hundred percent Republican. At this election, Rhodes became the first mayor in twenty years to win re-election. There were no elected Democrats in city hall and Rhodes was quick to say, "This place is the center of Republicanism in the state."

In his second term, Rhodes won the reputation of

being a leader in state financial affairs. He spearheaded a drive of municipal officials to get more money returned to the cities from the state. He continued a busy schedule promoting athletics. His theme at the time was, "I feel the busy boy is a good boy, and a good boy is the best investment that you can make."

He expanded the police and fire departments. He implemented a lifelong practice of watchdog tactics on administration and expenditures in the bureaus and departments of his administration. He established three short rules for those working with him: "No drinking on the job, no hands in the till, no romancing the help." He insisted that all of the employees—including himself—follow these rules throughout his political career. Breaking one of these rules was the same as a resignation. If you broke the rules, you either resigned or were fired.

*P*eople learned to trust Rhodes. Throughout his political life he never took a bribe or built wealth on the basis of his years in political office.

In 1950, he made his first try for governor. He ran in the GOP primary in a field of four. The party choice was a GOP campaigner, Don H. Ebright, who had been elected Ohio Treasurer in 1940, 1942, 1944, 1946, and 1948. Rhodes ran second to Ebright, 338,390 to 157,346. He had run against the party choice in his first outing for ward committeeman sixteen years before. This was to be the last time that he was to run against party endorsement. His political purpose in 1950 was to start statewide recognition of his name. The Democratic candidate that year was Frank J. Lausche, who had been elected governor in 1944, was defeated in 1946, elected again in

1948, and was expected to win in 1950. He did so, beating Ebright by 150,000 votes. That was Rhodes' campaign number eight.

In 1951, at age 42, Rhodes was elected mayor for the third time. No Democrat opposed him, but Floyd Green tried again as an Independent. For this election, Rhodes piled up a sixty-four percent margin, 41,926 to 23,592. For the first time in twenty-four years—since 1927—a Columbus mayor had won a third term. During the 1952 campaign, when Rhodes ran for state auditor, James Allen, under his byline, summarized him as follows:

*When a candidate's platform sags, when his voice gets gravel rough haranguing voters with the same campaign clichés, Rhodes will give him a hand. He's quick to find a fault. Find an opponent's weakness and capitalize on it.*

*The phrase 'politician's politician' has been worked to death, but nothing better suits Rhodes. He is the best organization man in the party here and one of the best strategists. He's fearless and, if need be, ruthless. To him the party is paramount and if a head or two must drop to make it so, he has no qualms about using the ax.*

During his campaign for election as mayor, he was often asked, "Who is your campaign manager." He would reply, "My mother."

When people protested that his mother was not skilled as a campaign manager, he said, "She doesn't know all of the ins and outs of politics but she knows what's right and wrong."

During his years as mayor, Jim Rhodes:

- Cleaned up corruption in the city.
- Put the city on sound financial footing.
- Built Hoover Dam.
- Brought Westinghouse, General Motors, and the American Trotting Association to Columbus.
- Appointed the first African-American, Bill Anderson, to a cabinet position.
- Re-instituted rubbish collection after sixteen years.
- Sold King Avenue playground to Battelle, making its expansion in Columbus possible.
- Gave land to The Clintonville Women's Club.
- Brought Boy's Clubs to Columbus.
- Financed and built the first parking garage with parking meter money.
- Built Raymond Golf Course.
- Doubled the city park system.
- Brought the American Rose Society to Columbus and established a seventy-five acre rose garden.
- Built Veterans Memorial.
- Instituted a smoke abatement program.
- Instituted a successful program to destroy rats.
- Built swimming pools for the youth of the city.

These activities were made possible in part because faith in city hall was rekindled, leading to the passage of the city income tax and the 1945 passage of the $24,700,000 capital improvement bond issue and the 1951 bond issue of $23,188,100. Together, these issues won an additional $15,000,000 in federal grants.

⟶ Mayor Rhodes before leaving for the Olympics as member of the Olympics Committee.

While Rhodes was mayor, he continued to be a member of the U.S. Amateur Athletic Union, representing Ohio on that body. He attended the Olympic games before he was elected mayor of Columbus. He had attended the 1936 Olympics when Jesse Owens won four Gold Medals and embarrassed Adolph Hitler, the Chancellor of the Third Reich in Germany. Rhodes became acquainted with Jesse Owens and was instrumental in bringing him in contact with Alf Landon, who was running for president of the United States, and Jesse Owens supported Landon in the presidential race.

As the nations of the world prepared for the 1948 Olympics, Rhodes was elected to the U. S. Amateur Athletic Union. Avery Brundage was the head of the International Olympic Committee for the United States, and vice president of the full International Olympic Committee. The U. S. Amateur Athletic Union was a member of the International Sports Federation, and as its president, Rhodes was involved in discussions relating to the planning and operation of the Olympics.

His duties included both the pre-Olympic Games between the U.S. and British athletic teams as well as the International Olympic games that followed.

Rhodes was co-chairman of the U. S. vs. British games, and the other co-chairman was Charles, the Duke of Edinborough, husband of Queen Elizabeth the reigning Monarch of Britain. The U. S. vs. British Games were held in White City, England, one week prior to the International Olympic Games, and the U. S. won the pre-Olympic contest between the two countries, 13½ to 3 ½.

In order to qualify to participate in the Olympics, a nation had to be approved by the International Amateur Athletic Association. As president of the U. S. Amateur Athletic Association, Rhodes participated as a member of the International Association. Prior to the meeting of this Association to approve additional participants in the Olympics Game, Rhodes was contacted by Leon and Jerome Shottenstein, businessmen in Columbus, Ohio, asking that he encourage the International Athletic Federation to accept participants from Israel into the Olympic Games. Rhodes agreed and as Israel's participation in the Olympic Games came before this international federation, Avery Brundage opposed their participation.

⌐ The young mayor meets the elder statesman: When Winston Churchill came through Columbus in 1947 on the train, Rhodes went down to meet him and Churchill offered Rhodes a cigar. Rhodes said he didn't smoke. Churchill then pulled out a flask and offered the mayor a drink of whiskey. Rhodes said he didn't drink. Sniffed Churchill, "You'll never get anywhere as a politician."

As president of the U. S. Amateur Athletic Association, however, Rhodes strongly supported the participation of Israel.

Speaking before the gathered representatives from the entire nation, he pointed out the purpose of the games was brotherhood and that if a nation could be kept out because it was not liked by another nation there would be no International Olympic games. The vote was overwhelmingly in favor of Israel's participation.

As Israel was in the middle of a civil war, the athletes from that country arrived in fatigue clothes. The athletes from Israel who participated won only one medal, but the participation gave that fledgling nation a point of pride.

Rhodes, as President of the AAU, led one of the units of athletes on the opening march into the Olympic Arena.

When Rhodes returned to Columbus, the B'nai B'rith had a celebration in his honor. A park in Israel was created in his honor and he visited Israel to dedicate the park.

The United States won the 1948 Olympics with a score of thirty-eight gold, twenty-four silver, and twenty bronze medals. Sweden was second with seventeen gold, eleven silver, and sixteen bronze medals. Mike Peppe's swimmers did extremely well in the contests and after the final race the swimmers, in a spirit of jubilation, threw Peppe into the pool. They had to jump in and pull him out because he couldn't swim.

Soon after Rhodes was elected mayor for the third time, he ran for state auditor and won that election. He resigned as mayor to take on the new responsibility.

He left the city, as he would leave the state, well financed, with the budget in balance. His terms as mayor did not make him wealthy, but they did prove that an honest, people-centered, bold and hardworking innovator could be accepted and supported by the voters.

The spirit and pattern of his innovations, and his swift and courageous fight against gambling and crime were to be key factors in his later service as governor of Ohio.

In 1950, Roger W. Tracy who had run twice for state auditor against Joe Ferguson and lost, switched his goal to the office of state treasurer (being vacated by James Ebright) and won. This left the Ohio Auditor's race of 1952 open for the GOP. The party offered the nomination to Rhodes, as the unopposed candidate. His effective service as three-time mayor of Columbus earned him the respect of the party leadership.

Rhodes' success as Columbus mayor was summarized in an introduction to a 1993 monograph entitled, *A Tough Mayor for Hard Times,* honoring Rhodes on the fiftieth anniversary of his mayoral election. Gregory S. Lashutka, then mayor of Columbus, wrote:

*We in Columbus enjoy the quality of life and the economic power of a mighty city today, but it was not always so. Fifty years ago the opposite was true, with corruption like gambling and prostitution rampant, and city government in serious financial trouble. Columbus of the early Forties looked like anything but the growth-city of the future, the city to become Ohio's largest. At that critical moment in our city's history the race for mayor attracted an energetic young candidate who, like Columbus, was destined for greatness. He won, and in the ensuing ten years the foundation was laid for much of what Columbus is today. James Allen Rhodes was elected mayor November 2, 1943. This brief narrative history describes the Rhodes years as mayor on this, the fiftieth anniversary of his election.*

# Moving on up

It was obvious that in 1952 Joseph T.
Ferguson was going to run for re-election for his
Ohio Auditor office in spite of his 1950 drubbing
by Robert A. Taft for the U. S. Senate. Rhodes
had been calling the office the "catbird seat" of
the statehouse. He believed it was the path to
the governor's office. The office provided name
recognition and direct contact in every courthouse,
city hall, school board, and library in the state.

Rhodes did not initially have a long-range plan for
his career that involved running for auditor of the state
of Ohio. He became involved in a controversy with
Auditor Joe Ferguson over the purchase of coal for the
city of Columbus. Rhodes had purchased about $22,000
of coal on the open market because coal was short and
the power for the city and heat for state buildings was
in jeopardy. He had the support of the city council for
the purchase.

The Rhodes' daughters, Susan, Saundra, and Sharon, hit the campaign trail in 1954.

Ferguson raised serious questions about the purchases and made a personal finding against Rhodes and the city for the coal purchases. Rhodes vigorously fought the finding, blaming the inefficiencies of Ferguson's office for the problem. Rhodes pointed out the large number of relatives that Ferguson had employed in the auditor's office. Joe Ferguson was well-liked and firmly entrenched in the office.

During the battle over the findings, Ferguson wrote to Rhodes and said that if Rhodes was so smart, "Why don't *you* run for auditor?"

Challenged by this statement, Rhodes ran in the next election. It was a hard-fought election but Rhodes found out that Ferguson had purchased a new car for the auditor's office and planned to drive it to Florida to visit a relative. There wasn't any state business involved in the trip, and Rhodes notified the editors of the newspapers about the misuse of the state vehicle.

The news media met Ferguson as he arrived in Florida, and he quickly returned to Ohio. The damage was done, however, and the newspapers over the state roasted Ferguson for his indiscretion.

The ballot in the 1952 election year was headed by Dwight D. Eisenhower, who carried Ohio by 500,000 votes, followed by the governor's race where Frank Lausche (D) beat Charles P. Taft (R) by over 400,000 votes. Rhodes won the election by over 300,000 votes and moved to that office.

From this experience, he learned that an elected official should, "Never challenge another person to run for the office you hold," as Ferguson had challenged Rhodes.

As auditor, Rhodes again had the opportunity to learn where all the bodies were buried and where there was misfeasance and malfeasance of the fiscal offices over the state. The auditor's office has the responsibility to do pre and post audits of expenditures by state and local political divisions of the state. In carrying out his responsibilities, Rhodes was not interested in prosecuting individuals or offices for small discrepancies in expenditure of funds. Instead, he focused on getting the money back from those who had made errors, for the benefit of the taxpayer. Any criminal act, however, was prosecuted to the fullest.

His reasonable and honest approach to the administration of the auditor's office won him many friends and supporters in both parties. He updated the operation of the office and hired people on the basis of their competencies, rather than on their basis of family relationship or friendship.

While he was auditor, he established the Teenage Hall of Fame. He researched and identified the people reared in Ohio who had become famous before they were 18 years old. He set up a wall outside of the auditor's office, with pictures of all those who had achieved that status and invited Jesse Owens to dedicate the Hall of Fame. Jesse Owens was not able to attend but sent his daughter, a beautiful young lady.

As any youth group would come through the office on visits to the Capitol, Rhodes would meet them in the hall and extol the virtues of the youth that had become famous, from Newark's Johnny Clem, the 9 year old who ran away to join the Civil War and became a drummer boy, to Rhodes' friend Jesse Owens, who as an OSU track athlete broke three world records and tied a fourth, all in one afternoon in Michigan.

Rhodes' interest in youth was evidenced throughout his long political career, from Si-U through his four terms as governor. His interests included his own children and grandchildren, and their activities were the only things that caused him to turn down a political or governmental activity.

In 1954, Rhodes had completed two years of a four-year term. There was no one in the Republican Party who wanted to run against Frank Lausche. Since he was in a safe position, Rhodes ran against Lausche and lost by 210,000 votes out of 2.6 million cast. It was one of his few political losses.

In 1956, Lausche ran for the senate against George Bender, who was finishing out Robert A. Taft's last term. This left the governor's office wide open, but William O'Neill moved first to run for governor and Rhodes backed off and ran for re-election as state auditor. O'Neill was elected governor and Rhodes beat Joe Ferguson— again—by 300,000 votes.

In 1958, O'Neill lost to Mike DiSalle because of the

controversy over the "Right to Work Law" and most Republicans went down to defeat. Rhodes ran again in 1960 for the two-year term as auditor, when the term of office was shortened to two years for one election so that all state offices would be on a four-year basis. Again, Rhodes won by a large margin, which placed him in position to run for governor in 1962.

His three terms as auditor were marked by the hallmarks that marked his entire career—honesty, competence, and dedication to the public.

On September 13, 1962, James A. Rhodes was 53 years old. It had been thirty years since he had moved to Columbus from Springfield. He was ready for his fourteenth campaign since his 1934 start, winning the ward committeeman job. For four years Rhodes, as auditor of Ohio, had kept close tabs on Governor DiSalle's administration. The economy was soft and Ohio unemployment was up. As governor, DiSalle had increased taxes, including an added two cents per gallon to the gasoline tax. The interstate system was under construction but the people were impatient for it. The state was a big traffic jam, with unemployment and new taxes bugging the voters. It was a time ripe for change.

In the spring primary, Governor DiSalle was politically wounded with a challenge from Democrat regular Mark McElroy, who four years before had beaten William Saxbe in the race for Ohio Attorney General. The primary race fatally split the Democrats. DiSalle, the incumbent governor, won the Democratic primary with just over fifty percent of his party's vote. Rhodes was opposed in the primary by William I. White but it was no contest. Rhodes, clearly his party's choice, won the spring primary with 520,868 votes to White's 59,916.

The campaign found Rhodes at factory gates, union halls, churches, county fairs, athletic events, newspaper offices, board rooms, association meetings, chamber of commerce luncheons, schools, colleges, and standing at the end of unfinished highways—wherever and whenever people gathered or could be gathered. He was omnipresent at GOP functions and fund-raisers for himself and other Republican candidates. It was the beginning of the unique "Rhodes Constituency," a combination of traditional Republicans supplemented by the swing voters among housewives, working families, church members, farmers, professionals, businessmen, and special interests—such as contractors. From one point of view he put the silent majority together long before the term was popular.

The repetitive themes of the 1962 Rhodes campaign were built around the "jobs and progress" program of his successful administration as mayor of Columbus and now applied directly to the 1962 situation. For example, the DiSalle administration agency for generating new jobs In Ohio was the Department of Industrial and Economic Development, an acronym of which is DIED. Rhodes campaign speeches included the imperative "DIED is dead—Dead as a Dodo." He also coined the phrase, *Profit is Not a Dirty Word in Ohio*. While radio and TV spots were used, they were not the major factor. Basically, it was a campaign of making the rounds, from Labor Day until the Monday before election.

James A. Rhodes was elected governor of Ohio for the first time on November 7, 1962, by a plurality of over 550,000 votes—nearly fifty-nine percent of all the votes cast. He led the ticket and carried into office every other Republican candidate except for Frank Lausche, who was re-elected to the U.S. Senate. One of the Republicans elected was Robert Taft Jr., running on his first state ballot as congressman at-large.

The economy in Ohio was weak and the budget proposal for the new biennium was not in balance. Rhodes had appointed Richard Krabach as director of finance and Howard Collier as his assistant. There probably has never been a stronger or more competent team in that office before or since. Director Krabach recommended to the governor that the total number of state employees be reduced by ten percent. Two days after Rhodes took office, the directive was put into action. There was a great amount of opposition but the directive held and the budget was balanced.

In the two months between his election and inauguration, Rhodes not only laid out his programs for higher education, transportation, recreation, economic development, and aid to the aged, he had his appointed team named and in place. As Tom Dudgeon said in the introduction to *Ohio's Governor of the Century*:

"His plan was clear: Build the facilities and the people will use them, solving their own social needs. He did it on the "pay as you use (bond finance)" rather than the "pay as you build (more taxes)" basis. In the process, he changed the face of Ohio forever and became the most important influence of Ohio's twentieth century.

"His greatest gift is the gift of timing that is not captured in these pages. Over the years, even his enemies developed a grudging respect for his political genius, as the 'boy wonder' of Columbus City Hall and later as the fox of the Ohio Statehouse. His staff appointments throughout the sixteen years were competent, clean, and loyal to Ohio. His relationship with the general assembly was marked by open communication and general cooperation.

"Among his real accomplishments were a few cockamamie schemes and he was a master of the non-answer to press questioning when it suited him. Ohioans are also reckless by nature and given to dreams of a brighter tomorrow. We liked a governor with a few crazy ideas which made us feel good and laugh a bit."

*D*uring his first term Rhodes proposed—and the people of Ohio passed—a bond issue to push ahead the completion of the interstate highway system. The issue was of major importance to Rhodes in building industry and jobs in Ohio.

His first administration went well. By 1966, the Ohio economy had become stronger and, month after month, the interstate roads were beginning to be opened. Times were good and Rhodes had medicated the bruises of the Ohio conservatives. The 1966 election campaign, number sixteen for Rhodes, was over almost before it began. Frazier Reams Jr., a Democrat from Toledo, was the challenger for governor.

It was a small election, with about 2.9 million voting. Rhodes was elected with a 700,000 plurality, sixty-two percent of the vote. Again, he carried into office the entire slate of Republican GOP statewide non-court candidates. Rhodes' coattails were long and any Republican candidate was welcomed aboard if the candidate thought the coattail would help him. If the candidate did not believe Rhodes' assistance would be of help, Rhodes stayed out of his district.

During the second term, a special statewide election had become necessary to offer a constitutional amendment to provide a method of apportionment of the house of representatives and the senate. Rhodes saw this as an opportunity to present to the voters a capital improvement financing method that would also require a constitutional amendment. The method proposed would support Rhodes' concept of "pay as you use," rather than "pay as you build."

The idea was to create a state bonding commission with authority to consolidate state bonded indebtedness under legislatively earmarked general revenues backed by the full faith and credit of the state. Under the proposal, the state legislature would authorize the capital improvements for education, office buildings, prisons, hospitals or otherwise—within the authorized bonding capacity—then the bonding commission would fund the projects by establishing bond terms and issues. Simplistically, it proposed to create a state development bank to finance state-owned construction through mortgage financing. It was an extension of a Rhodes system of public financing which he had used successfully as both mayor and governor for government "brick and mortar."

The trouble at the ballot box was that the idea was unacceptable to the public. In a vote of 1.5 million it went down by 500,000 votes. It even carried the reapportionment amendment down to defeat, which had to be redrawn and submitted again the following November. That version passed handily.

In the eyes of the news media, the campaign for the Ohio Bond Commission was Rhodes', and the news media generally opposed the idea. This marked the

⌐The Governor and Helen
on her 60th birthday.

turning point in the rapport between Rhodes and the
working press, which thereafter claimed the size of his
1966 election success had been used to try to "put one
over" on the public. In retrospect, however, given the
subsequent inflation and the obvious use of the same
financial plan to rescue New York City from operational
bankruptcy, the OBC proposal was neither fiscally nor
administratively imprudent. It was a political defeat,
however, and would color the press coverage of Rhodes'
next election.

In the 1968 presidential election, Ohio went for Nixon
by 90,000 votes over Humphrey. Bill Saxbe led the Ohio
GOP ticket, beating John Gilligan for the U.S. Senate by
100,000 votes. One issue on the ballot was an amendment
to allow bonds to be issued for highways and other capital

improvements. It passed by over 200,000 votes, which allowed the intent, if not the method, of the ill-fated OBC to go forward for the rest of the Rhodes administration.

Summary of James A. Rhodes' first eight years, 1963–1971

**Education:** More revenue provided for elementary and secondary school than during the entire period 1916–1963, $3.2 billion compared to $2.9 billion. Included was $70 million to aid urban disadvantaged youth and $75 million for vocational education facility construction. College spending increased five-fold to $500 million. Also, $800 million invested for new construction as state universities increased from five to twelve.

The plan for providing vocational education through 120 vocational education districts, including all 720 school districts in the state, was completed.

Thirteen two-year post high school technical institutes, supported by industry, were in operation and growing rapidly as funds were provided at the request of the state board of regents for both program and buildings. The Division of Vocational Education, State Department of Education, with the strong support of Governor Rhodes had initiated this new development in education.

**Development:** Commercial and industrial facilities expansion attracted $13 billion in new capital investment. About 400 new firms moved into Ohio and 15,500 existing plants expanded operations, adding about 75,000 more jobs.

**Natural resources:** Developed one of the finest park and recreation systems in the nation. More than $113 million invested in new capital improvements. Added about 50,000 acres of public land and 8,600 acres of new impounded waters.

**Mental hygiene:** Started phase-out from large institutions to smaller, community-based mental health centers. Six such centers were completed during his administrations and two were started. Improved treatment methods that reduced institution population from 22,150 to 15,031 in 1970. Nearly $2 million in grants for expended senior citizens projects.

**Corrections:** Established Adult Parole Authority and expanded parole and probation services and the inmate population cut. Started construction of penitentiary in Scioto County.

**Health:** New sewage treatment facilities increased: 389 projects costing $117 million approved by health department in 1969.

Streamlined the administration by creating five districts under deputy directors. Funds hiked from $100 million in 1963 to $225 million in fiscal 1970.

State laws on farming modernized. Cooperative agreement with the federal department assured wholesome meat products to Ohio consumers. New $620,000 laboratory aimed at improved consumer protection at Reynoldsburg.

**Historical:** Led in preservation of historical sites and memorabilia. Built new Ohio Historical Center on state fair ground. It opened in August, 1970. Also added eight topical state museums.

**Highway safety:** Traffic fatalities sank to about seventy percent below national average, while vehicle registrations soared to 6.5 million. Highway patrolman increased from 862 to 1120.

**Industrial safety:** Several new job safety programs launched, including special emphasis on supervisors training course by employers to train 26,924 in the eight-year period.

**Public works:** A total of $694,799,162 of new public works construction placed under contract with 180 more contracts estimated at $350 million in design.

**Employment services:** Lowest unemployment rate of any industrial state. Unemployment compensation trust fund in sound financial condition, showing a balance of $700 million, compared to $68 million in April 1963.

**Commerce:** County airport program initiated to attract industry. Ninety-three were capable of handling industrial jets in 83 of the 99 counties.

**Urban affairs:** This Department created by the Rhodes administration participated in the development of federal-state aid programs in low-income housing and anti-poverty training programs. Creation of Appalachian office resulted in Ohio receiving $90,577,453.00 for programs to stimulate economic growth in 28-county region of Southeastern Ohio.

**Liquor control:** Conducted one of the nation's most vigorous programs against juvenile drinking, gambling, nudity, and obscenity. Total of $396.6 million transferred into the state general fund from profit of operating 370 liquor outlets. Sales were at an all-time high of $319 million in 1969.

**Personnel:** Ohio had the fewest state employees per capita of any state. The rate of minimum pay for state workers increased fifty-eight percent, from $1.82 an hour to $2.88.

**Highways:** The highway system was credited with drawing several billions of dollars of new and expanded industry to Ohio. Total of $3.3 billion worth of highways placed under contract. The interstate system brought to a total of 1,390 miles open to traffic

**Youth commission:** Provided more capital improvement funds for youth facilities— $16,667,000.00—than in the previous fifty years.

**Finance:** Moved the state from $83 million debt and unpaid bills to steadily balanced budgets. When Rhodes left office, all bills were paid and spending continued at then current levels was expected to produce budget surplus of about $10 million on June 30, 1971.

**Cabinet members, first eight years:**

*Executive Assistant*, John McElroy, 1963–70
*Adjutant General*, Erwin C. Hostetler, 1963–68;
    Sylvester Del Corso, 1969–70

*Agriculture,* John Stackhouse
*Commerce,* Warren Chase 1963–64; J. Gordon
  Peltier, 1965–70
*Development,* Fred P. Neuenschwander
*Finance,* Richard L. Krabach, 1963–1968; Howard
  L.Collier 1969–70
*Health,* Emmett W. Arnold
*Highway Safety,* Warren C. Nelson
*Highways,* Pearl E. Masheter
*Industrial Relations,* William O. Walker
*Insurance,* William R. Morris
*Liquor Control,* Donald D. Cook
*Mental Hygiene,* Martin A. Janis
*Natural Resources,* Fred E. Morr
*Personnel,* Wayne Ward
*Public Utilities Commission,* Carl R. Johnson
*Public Welfare,* Denver L. White
*Public Works,* Alfred C. Gienow
*Taxation,* Gail Porterfield
*Unemployment Compensation,* Willard P. Dudley
*Urban Affairs,* Albert G. Giles, 1969–70
*Workman's Compensation,* Jay C. Flowers
*Ohio Youth Commission,* Wayne Fogle, 1965–66;
  Daniel W. Johnson, 1967–70

After eight years as govenor, Rhodes could not run again, and in 1970 he decided to run for the Senate seat vacated by Stephen Young. Both Robert Taft and Rhodes ran for the Republican nomination for the U.S. Senate. There were 970,000 Republican votes cast in the primary election and at least 30,000 chose not to vote for either the senator or the governor.

The day before the May 4, 1970, election, Rhodes called up the National Guard to deal with protest violence at Kent State University. The tragic outcome of that forty-fifth call-up was the Kent State tragedy. The event may have accounted for the fact that Taft won the GOP primary election by 5,270 votes out of the 940,000 votes cast. Rhodes always declined that excuse, saying, "The governor has a role in the protection of life and property. He cannot shun it when the occasion demands he play it."

Taft won the fall election to the U.S. Senate and John Gilligan became governor. For the first time since 1934, James A. Rhodes was not in an elected public office. Rhodes, unlike other politicians who stayed in office for many years, did not leave office a rich man. After all the years in public office at both city and state level, his total worth was $65,000. He left the office a relatively poor man but he left both Columbus and Ohio physically, socially and economically well and healthy. As he left, he told a supporter, "When (not if) I come back, I will not need any other person's money. "

# The latter innings

Almost two years to the day after he left office, Rhodes started his seventeenth campaign with the objective of regaining the governor's office. The reason for the early start was the constitutional amendment passed in 1959 that stated: "No person shall hold the office of governor for a period longer than two successive terms of four years."

Rhodes' strategy was to file more than a year early in order to permit time before the election for court litigation that could decide if the amendment would prohibit him from running for governor after being out of office for a term. His position was that the amendment did not prevent a person from serving as governor for additional terms, as long as there were no more than two successive terms.

In January 1973, Rhodes filed petitions containing enough valid signatures with the secretary of state. They were rejected, enabling Rhodes to carry a challenge to the Ohio Supreme Court. On May 10, 1973, the court ruled that "two successive terms" did not prevent a person from running for governor for additional terms, if he was out of office for one or more terms. Even with his early

Governor Rhodes (left)
with Richard Nixon, circa 1971.

announcement, Rhodes was behind Governor Gilligan, who announced on December 2, 1972, his intention to seek re-election.

The announcements did not automatically assure either candidate the nomination in November of 1974. Animosities and internal strife were embedded in both political parties and both Rhodes and Gilligan were directly involved. The political wounds to Rhodes were older. They stemmed partly from the protests of the 1960s—the bias of the young, liberal, anti-establishment reporters—as well as the criticism of GOP conservatives about Rhodes' lack of purity as a "real Republican," and the disenchanted patronage seekers who exist for any senior politician after years in office. Rhodes, however, worked hard at overcoming these obstacles. Gilligan's political wounds were not only fresh, but were constantly being reopened.

Both Rhodes and Gilligan were challenged for their party's nomination in the May, 1974, primary. Rhodes had two contenders, Charles Fry of Springfield, a state representative, former state senator, and contractor. The other was Bert Dawson Jr., Columbia County engineer. Gilligan faced a challenge from gadfly James D. Nolan, a Cleveland nursing home operator.

*R*hodes won the party nomination without engaging in any inter-party brawling. He drew 385,669 votes to Charles Fry's 183,889 and Dawson's 44,938. Gilligan won the Democratic nomination with 713,488 votes to Nolan's 294,938. More important, John Glenn won the nomination for the U.S. Senate over John Gilligan's choice for the seat, Howard Metzenbaum.

Between the primary in the spring and the November election, the Watergate horrors peaked to a presidential resignation and the Republicans were expected to go down in defeat. During the primary, Rhodes' theme was consistently, "Remember how good the eight years were when I governed before, and how much we did for Ohio. We managed. Gilligan mismanaged. The issue is Gilligan's management credibility."

Rhodes' campaign tactics were critical to his seventeenth campaign. Early in the campaign he decided to use commercial television—campaign spots to "leap" directly to his populist "swing votes" among the average Ohioans. Those who had voted for him for governor in 1962, when they were 21 years old, were in their mid-30s in 1974 and involved in raising families. They were also TV watchers. The new 19-year-old voters also received their news from the TV.

Rhodes picked a small campaign staff and aimed his limited funds toward TV-radio ads through a respected campaign agency, Bailey, Deardourf & Frye, Inc., of Washington, D.C. Early in June, Rhodes announced to the party leaders and contributors that he would need a million dollars to fund his autumn efforts.

During the days when Gilligan was remaining "above the struggle" as governor, the Rhodes' TV ads were five-minute, semi-biographical spots. The theme was "Remember how good it was." When the Gilligan campaign switched to personal attacks—as Rhodes expected they would—he had his TV blitz ready to go onto all 226 AM and FM stations and the twenty-six commercial TV stations. They were all professionally prepared messages built to re-emphasize those Gilligan scars.

The Gilligan campaign was built around the old "door step" political technique. His campaign had forty full-time, eighty part-time employees, and 40,000 volunteers. Rhodes had six full-time and two part-time aides for his campaign staff.

Gilligan spent over a million dollars and received 1,482,191 votes at a cost of 69.7 cents each. Rhodes, meanwhile, spent $856,749.19 and received 1,493,679 votes at a cost of 57.4 cents each

Both candidates received totals well under their previous record. After the Watergate debacle, people were sick of politics. There were fewer voters participating than in the 1962 election. The difference was not in the excitement for the candidates, it was the campaign tactics. After the elections, Gilligan said, "I was relying on 40,000 to turn out the vote. ...They had a pitch, you know, on-the-door step with a little piece of literature. But Deardourf was in their living room (on television) fifteen times a day, beating hell out of them, and it was not an even match."

*I*n January of 1975, James A. Rhodes, at 65, became the governor of Ohio for the third four-year term. This time, however, he was not able to provide coattails for other Republicans. Only one other Republican got into office, incumbent Ted Brown, the secretary of state. Even the lieutenant governor's job went to Gilligan's hand picked candidate—Richard Celeste, a young Cleveland legislator.

One incident that occurred as a part of this hard-fought election illustrated another of Rhodes' strengths in the political arena. As the evening of election wore on, the returns pointed to a victory for Governor Gilligan. Near midnight, Rhodes called a news conference and gave a speech conceding defeat, congratulating Gilligan on his victory and wishing him well in his next term. Rhodes then went to bed. He had done his best and thought he had lost. He had no time for recriminations and could go to sleep with a clear conscience. He awoke the next morning to find that he had been elected the governor of Ohio for his third term.

This typified Rhodes in any conflict of ideas. Do your best, but if it is not to be, move on to the next opportunity or item of business. Don't waste time or energy on a lost cause. Live to fight another day.

Rhodes' eighteenth campaign was for re-election in 1978 for a fourth term as governor. The Democrats began staking out the territory early. Their candidate was to be the young lieutenant governor and his campaign began in earnest with Rhodes's last attempt to establish his capital improvement financing ideas as a major program.

Almost as soon as the 1974 recount was over, Rhodes determined that in order for Ohio to afford a capital improvement program, increase funding for education, and meet the effects of inflation on the state budgets without raising taxes, there would have to be some financial maneuvering. There was also another cycle of high unemployment.

When he went to the general assembly, both houses were in Democrat control. He asked for a tax abatement for industry and three bond issues: for inner city rebuilding; highway improvements; and housing. None of the four got through the legislature, so Rhodes took the unusual step of placing each on initiative petitions that required a voter referendum. Signatures were collected and the issues were submitted at an off-year election. All four were defeated badly. The newspaper opposition was old 1967 rhetoric against the Ohio Bond Commission.

The state official who assumed the role of vocal antagonist was Lieutenant Governor Richard F. Celeste, and following the defeat, Celeste's office became an active center for criticism of Governor Rhodes, as well as the campaign center for "Celeste for Governor."

During that time, Celeste also made the rounds of party functions throughout the state. By primary time, now June, Celeste had no viable Democrat opponent for his party's nomination.

Not so for Rhodes, however. In the 1978 primary, Charles F. Kurfess, the former Republican Speaker of the Ohio House, challenged Rhodes. The vote was 393,632 for Rhodes and 187,544 for Kurfess. There were more voting on the Republican ticket, however, than there were Democrats voting in the primary—forty-three percent fewer Democrats voting than in the 1974 election.

Celeste, as Rhodes saw it, was a Gilligan disciple who had leap-frogged other Democrat candidates, primarily with the help of the liberal protesters of the 1960s. Rhodes

Governor Rhodes with Gerald Ford
during Ford's run for the Presidency in the 1970s.

believed that Celeste would not go down well with Ohio's industrial-minded "silent majority."

He knew both intuitively and by experience there are two kinds of liberalism in American politics. There is the New Deal version of the 1930s and 1940s aimed at working Americans and based on jobs for all with subsidies as necessary. There is also the 1960s version, the Great Society and War on Poverty, aimed at intellectual liberals and based on redistributing wealth.

Rhodes own "Jobs and Progress" theme over the years was and is an obvious endorsement of the role of government in preventing and abating unemployment. From his substantial support from working Ohioans, he also knew that the second kind of liberalism is often seen by working people as actually subsidizing and perpetuating joblessness. Rhodes saw this difference between his own record and the "new liberalism" theme of the Celeste campaigners as the 1978 issue.

There was another low vote year in 1978, when barely 3,000,000 voted. Rhodes was again the winner, by nearly 50,000 votes. It was a slim margin, and again Democrats carried the other statewide offices, this time toppling even the veteran secretary of state, Ted W. Brown.

Rhodes was 68 years old and although the campaigners continued to say "age is not a factor," it was in the minds of the voters. The governor could still outpace the press corps on the campaign, even though it had been thirty-six years since he had won his first statewide election. The young families voting then were now grandparents getting ready to retire, and many of them believed "Old Jim" should do likewise.

It was generally agreed the swing votes, which carried the day for Rhodes, occurred the weekend before the Tuesday election or in the voting booth itself. Again, TV use may have been the reason. The TVs that weekend carried spots of Rhodes leading a rousing rendition of the "Battle Hymn of the Republic" by the State Fair Boys Band and Choir. It was a masterpiece put together at the last hour and seemed to convince the Silent Majority, "to give it to Jim again."

Summary of Rhodes' second eight years, 1975–1983

**Education:** The University of Cincinnati became a state institution. Two new two-year colleges were added (Edison and Southern), The Ohio University Osteopathic

College created, and the Cancer Research Center added at The Ohio State University.

Funding for vocational education was tripled and 800 percent more students served by vocational education. The system of vocational education achieved 98.6 percent of the goal to make an adequate program available to all youth in Ohio. Over forty percent of all the students in the last two years of high school were enrolled in vocational programs. The same facilities used for the vocational educational education of youth also served over 250,000 adults for training for new jobs or the upgrading of their skills in their present job.

Funding for special education, youth with physical handicaps or learning disabilities increased 127 percent. Local aid increased only 45 percent.

Two-year technical education programs and enrollments continued to grow and more of the technical institutes became community colleges.

**Public works:** The state EPA provided over $600 million to local governments in wastewater treatment grants, in contrast with only $18 million in 1973 and 1974.

Financed over $380 million for clean air and clean water projects.

**Finance:** Implementation of cost control recommendations that saved the state over $100 million, two-thirds of which recur every year.

**Development:** Ohio gained 481,000 new jobs between 1975 and 1980. Gains in jobs were recorded in all areas of employment, manufacturing, non-manufacturing, retail and distribution, and research.

Honda and Ford located in Ohio because of strong effort and innovations by the administration.

Promoted Ohio's vast coal reserves and development off the fluidized bed and other processes to burn it cleanly and efficiently.

Developed and implemented self-help in order to encourage Ohio industry to use Ohio's cheap and available natural gas.

Created a cabinet-level energy department and pushed energy concerns to the forefront in Ohio.

**Natural resources:** Expanded the park system by adding Maumee Bay Park, West Branch Park, East Fork Park, Cleveland Waterfront Park, and Alum Creek Park.

Established the Ohio Village on land at the Ohio State fair grounds.

**Mental hygiene:** The state placed emphasis on patient treatment at the community level. State institution population decreased by twenty-nine percent.

All mental health/retardation facilities were accredited by the end of 1978.

Twenty percent of all community health facilities in the country were located in Ohio.

**Health:** The Industrial Commission and Rehabilitation Services Commission developed two comprehensive work rehabilitation centers, one in Cleveland and one in Columbus.

Initiated programs run by the physically handicapped for the physically handicapped, which placed 5,600 physically handicapped people in productive jobs.

**Welfare:** Proposed and worked for passage of reduced utility rates for the elderly (Lifeline Bill). It resulted in a twenty-five percent reduction in utility bills for 281,000 elderly people.

Legislation expanding the homestead exemption eligibility from $2,000 to $7,000, proposed a further exemption to $15,000.

Complete reorganization of the welfare department for more efficient administration of welfare caseload.

**Personnel:** Fewer state employees.

Ohio had the lowest number of state employees per capita of any state in the country.

Proposed the first Sunset legislation.

Initiated the Golden Buckeye Card, used by 700,000 senior citizens in Ohio at the time, many more today.

**State buildings:** Built the Rhodes Tower office building to relieve shortage of office space for state departments, which eliminated payment for many rented facilities over the city. This office building is the tallest building in the city of Columbus.

Made plans and arranged funding for the Riffe Building that was completed in the term if the next governor.

**Cabinet members, second eight years:**

*Executive Assistant*, Thomas A. Moyer, 1975–78; Robert F. Howarth, 1979–82

*Adjutant General*, James C. Clem, !975–82

*Administrative Services*, Richard L. Krabach, 1975–76; William W. Wilkins 1977–82

*Agriculture*, John Stackhouse, !975–82

*Office of Budget & Management*, Howard L. Collier,
      1975–76, 1981–82; William D. Kelp, 1977–80

*Commerce*, J. Gordon Peltier, 1975–82

*Economic & Community Development*, James A.
      Duerk, 1975–82

*Employment Services*, Albert C Giles, 1975–81;
      Gary E. Stein 1982

*Energy*, Robert S. Ryan, 1975–81; Robert A.
      Masoner, 1982

*Environmental Protection Agency*, Ned E. Williams,
      1976; James F McAvoy, 1977–79; Wayne S.
      Nichols, 1980–82

*Health*, John H. Akerman, MD 1975–82

*Highway Safety*, Donald D. Cool, 1975–78; Robert
      M. Chiaramonte, 1979–80; Earl H. Reich,
      1981–82

*Industrial Commission*, Gregory J. Stebbins,
      1975–76

*Industrial Relations*, Helen Evans, 1975–82

*Insurance*, Harry V. Jump, 1975–80;
      Robert L. Patchford, 1981–82

*Liquor Control*, Clifford E. Reich, 1975–82

*Mental Health*, Timothy B. Moritz, 1975–82

*Natural Resources*, Robert W. Teater, 1975–82

*Youth Commission*, William K. Willis, 1975–82

*Public Utilities*, C. Luther Heckman, 1975

*Public Welfare*, Raymond F. McKenna, 1975–76;
      Kenneth B. Creasy, 1977–82

*Rehabilitation & Corrections*, George F. Denton,
      1975–82

*Tax Commissioner*, Edger L. Lindley, 1975–82

*Transportation*, Richard D. Jackson, 1975–77;
David L. Weir, 1978–82
*Workman's Compensation*, Kenneth E. Krouse,
1975–77; Robert C. Daugherty, 1978–82

## The last race

Having served another eight years as governor, Rhodes was not eligible to run in the 1982 race. In 1986, however, at age 76 and convinced the Celeste administration was engaged in self-serving practices at the expense of Ohio's well being, Rhodes decided to run for the governor's office a fifth time.

When asked by the press the reason why, he quipped, "I get up early in the morning anyway."

Referring to Rhodes' campaign schedule an aide said, "That's why he is running again. He enjoys it."

Initial surveys in the northeast, made with Ohio business executives, showed that Rhodes was the preferred candidate.

The survey results:
*Rhodes—44.2%*
*Celeste—30.2%*
*Pfeifer—10.9%*
*Kucinich—4.9%*
*Gilmor—9.8%*

After the primary (Kucinich withdrew under party pressure) and by the date of the *Columbus Dispatch* first poll, Rhodes was favored by forty-eight percent of the respondents and Celeste by forty-three.

The GOP primary election fatally damaged Rhodes, who had forty-eight percent of the party's 731,000 votes. Celeste, however, had polled 600,000 of his

Rhodes meets with the new governor, Dick Celeste, in 1983.

party's primary votes while running unopposed. The challenge was obvious; Rhodes would need to win more Democrat votes than he had in the last two elections. This meant money, since Celeste's war chest had been active throughout his four years.

The Rhodes' fund-raisers never reached the point of competitiveness, even though he loaned $359,000 of his own funds to the effort. The general re-election campaign report tells the whole story. Celeste spent $4,077,655 on his re-election effort and ended with an unexpended balance of $860,445. Rhodes spent $1,959,572 (forty-eight percent of the Celeste amount), and ended with an unpaid loan of $100,000 that he forgave.

At the polls, Celeste was the big winner with 1,854,304 votes to Rhodes' 1,206,854. During the campaign

Rhodes was forced to suspend his activities when his wife became seriously ill. The *Cleveland Plain Dealer's* post election wrap-up observed that Celeste waged a cleverly crafted campaign that highlighted his political strengths and obscured his political vulnerabilities.

Most of the credit for Celeste's big win must go to Rhodes, who was unable to buy TV ads. Rhodes had been outgunned.

# *You win with people*

Like Woody Hayes, the Buckeye football
coach, Rhodes believed that one should:

*Pick good people.*

*Motivate them to come up with ideas that would improve
the services of government.*

*Provide them with moral and fiscal support.*

*Hold their feet to the fire to insure performance.*

In all of his terms as governor, he had the
members of his cabinet selected and in place before
he took the oath of office.

He selected good people and they followed the
three basic rules that he set out for his staff or they
were "unselected." The three rules were the same as he
had used when he was mayor of Columbus:

> *No drinking on the job.*
> *No romancing the help.*
> *No hands in the till.*

These rules were enforced regardless of the position of the staff member or his closeness to the governor.

A staff member, important to the operation of the governor's program, began staying in Columbus on weekends instead of going home to be with his wife. The governor found out he was having affairs at a Columbus hotel. The staff member was told to stop the practice and when he did not follow the advice, he was relieved of his office.

Another staff member was called into the office of the governor's personnel aide, Roy Martin.

"Have you ever taken Miss 'So and So' (a member of the man's clerical staff) home?" Martin asked.

"Yes, I have," the man answered.

"Have you ever gone into her house on these occasions?" Roy continued.

"Why, yes I have," the man said.

"Have you ever been in her bedroom?" Martin asked.

"I believe so."

"Have you ever been to bed with her?" Martin inquired.

"I don't believe that is any of your business," the man stated indignantly.

"Well, you might as well have," Martin said, "because you are fired."

It is not possible to give adequate recognition to the loyal members of the governor's staff who served over his sixteen years in office, but the great progress made in the Rhodes' years depended upon both the leader and the outstanding men and women that served him and Ohio. All were selected on the basis of their competence and all had the freedom to disagree with the governor

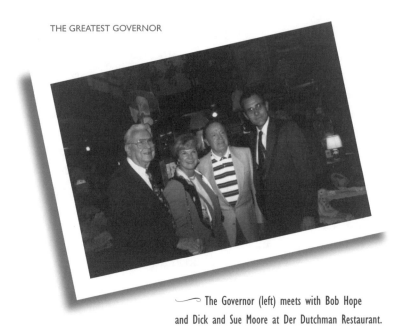

The Governor (left) meets with Bob Hope and Dick and Sue Moore at Der Dutchman Restaurant.

if they believed a project was not feasible. They all had the freedom to suggest new concepts or directions. The governor listened to his staffers and he motivated them with his many concepts for improving services to the people. He motivated them to think beyond the "what is" and "what has been."

It was difficult to overestimate the loyalty demonstrated by the group of people who served under the leadership of Governor James A. Rhodes. For the past several years—more than fifteen years after he left office—over a hundred former staff members and their spouses have gathered at Der Dutchman restaurant in Plain City, near Columbus, to honor Rhodes and remember and reminisce. No other governor ever enjoyed such a staff or engendered such loyalty.

Following are letters of appreciation written by Governor Rhodes' staff members:

# THE SUPREME COURT OF OHIO
30 EAST BROAD STREET,
COLUMBUS, OHIO 43266-0419

THOMAS J. MOYER
CHIEF JUSTICE

*April 26, 1999*

I had the privilege of serving as Executive Assistant to Governor Rhodes from 1975 to 1979. I soon realized that I was observing a man with a genius for understanding the expectation of citizens for their government; He derived his greatest satisfaction, not from making promises, but by producing results from action. I cannot imagine any other public official having a greater direct impact upon the lives of people than Governor Rhodes.

Finally, and most importantly, I was never requested in four years to do something that I believed improper. Governor Rhodes had a keen sense of right and wrong, fairness, and unfairness, and it influenced all of his decisions. Today, I continue to apply much of what I observed and learned from Ohio's greatest political figure.

Sincerely,

Thomas J. Moyer

# HAMILTON & ASSOCIATES
## 88E BROAD STREET SUITE 2000
## COLUMBUS OHIO 43215

*March 25, 1999*

Although I knew the Governor several years before I began working for him, my first real working adventure was in 1967. I picked him up at the Cuyahoga County Airport; His entourage included Attorney General Saxbe, who was running for senate; son-in-law Dick Moore; and first grandchild, Missy. We were to visit the ski slope in Northeast Ohio. I had arranged to have lunch at a quiet restaurant but I quickly learned the Governor doesn't do "regular lunches."

"Get Missy a hot dog," said the Governor, "we have to move on." Throughout my many excursions with the Governor it's been fast food and move on to the next project. Although in his last decade it's "go to the Der (Der Dutchman in Plain City)."

When the Governor was re-elected in 1974, I was employed as the director of personnel for the city of Cleveland. The late Bob Hughes and I were best of friends: Bob told me Governor Rhodes wanted me to become personnel director for the state. After many hours of negotiation we finally agreed. I was concerned about leaving Cleveland, for my relationship with Mayor Ralph Perk was perfect, but he also believed it was a good opportunity for me and I was one of the few appointed from Cleveland. The Governor told me I would never want to go back to Cleveland after I had lived in Columbus and he was correct.

Shortly after inauguration the Governor contracted pneumonia. It was then I learned that he only had lunch that day and the new lieutenant governor was Richard Celeste of the opposite party.

As was common occurrence in those days, the Governor called one morning and asked me to walk over to his office. In the cabinet room he was talking with the Director of Aging, Martin Janis. They told me of a problem. They wanted to start the Golden Buckeye Program but the Democratic Legislature would not give any money.

Since I was responsible for the Comprehensive Employment Training Account (CETA) we were able to fund slots for people to sell the Golden Buckeye program to the business community. It has been hugely successful the past twenty years. The Governor developed new ideas with regularity. Many folks believed that he was at least twenty years ahead of everyone else because of his outstanding foresight.

—Phil Hamilton

# F.P. NEUENSCHWANDER & ASSOCIATES
## 618 SOUTH NINTH STREET
## COLUMBUS, OHIO 43206

James A. Rhodes was always a family man, devoting any spare time to be with his wife, children, and grandchildren.

He had a great love for Ohio and its citizens, working tirelessly to improve the economic and living conditions. Vision and ideas came naturally to him and through his tireless efforts truly great things were accomplished.

Much has been said about the Governor's outstanding achievements, which were more than all of the rest of Ohio's governors put together. Industrial development, parks, highways, airports, lodges, education were but a few of his priorities. One great area of achievement, which is not well documented, is in the field of International Trade. In 1965, Ohio started an office in Brussels, Belgium, one of the first that any state had opened.

The following year an office was opened in Tokyo, Japan, and soon after an office in Caracas, Venezuela. This was accomplished over the objections from the U. S. Department of State and Commerce. Later these two Departments applauded the idea of having states participate in foreign business.

Today, more than half of the fifty states have offices in Europe and Asia. During the 1970's, Governor Rhodes opened an office in Hubei Province of China. It was the only state office in China.

The fruits of these labors were to attract Honda and

its many suppliers to Ohio. During his years in office the Governor led numerous "business" trade missions to all parts of the world. These set a pattern for others to follow.

Bringing Honda to Ohio was truly a feat. At the start of their search for a location in the U.S., Honda's only choice was California. It had no knowledge of what Ohio was or where it was located. It was through persistence that the Governor and Mr. Honda became close friends. After many major discussions, both here and in Japan, Honda picked Marysville, Ohio. Of major importance in Honda's decision-making process was the accessibility of having the Ohio Transportation Research Center as a neighbor. Honda later purchased this huge research and testing facility.

It was Governor Rhodes who, with The Ohio State University, developed and orchestrated the concept for such a resource.

The development aspect of his administration was off to a fast start. Early in his first year in office a trip was made to St. Louis. In one day visits were made to Anheuser Busch, Ralston Perina and Wagner Electric. Each of the three companies visited that day committed themselves to Ohio. None of these companies had even considered Ohio. In fact, Rhodes was told that August Busch had already purchased land in Indiana for their new installation. In less than a half-hour a commitment was forthcoming from Mr. Busch for an Ohio facility. It was Governor Rhodes who was instrumental in enticing the National Football League Expansion Committee to select Cincinnati for a franchise. A passionate plea, by the Governor, in a New York meeting, turned the tables in favor of Ohio.

A unique, but outstanding administrative ability played a major role in Governor Rhodes' success. He had the ability to pull together an outstanding, dedicated staff and to allow them a free hand in the running of their operations. He definitely did not micro-manage state government. His leadership and enthusiasm gave inspiration and drive to all those around him. One of his favorite expressions told to his staff members, as they would leave his office, was "do something."

—Fred P. Neuenschwander
*(first director of development under Rhodes)*

# RHINHART, HOWARTH, RISHEL & KOPECH, LTD

*April 22, 1999*

*Governor James A. Rhodes*
*2375 Tremont Road*
*Upper Arlington, Ohio 43221*

Dear Governor:

I am writing to express my appreciation to you for making my life, the lives of my family and those of all Ohioans better. When it comes to judging past and future Governors, you are the benchmark against whom others will be measured.

I have so many wonderful memories of my days in the Governor's Office. So many occasions come to mind—so many people, who, if they could, would join in telling of their great respect for you: Roy Martin, Dick Krabach, Howard Collier, Dick Jackson, Wayne Nichols, Al Giles, on and on—so many great people!

I've heard it said over and over again, "Governor Rhodes picked good people and then stayed out of the way and let them do their jobs." But Governor, we both know that you knew, in detail, what each was doing and what was going on in every corner of Ohio. I remember you on the phone night after night, calling Ohioans around the state to "check in" and see how things were going in the communities.

Your insight, common sense, and dignity stand out in my mind. But even more your loyalty for the average, hard-working Ohioans stands out. I remember your Christmas-time speech when Ohio's economy was being devastated by historically high national interest rates and unemployment. You addressed the members of the General Assembly, urging them to pass much needed taxes. There was never a question in your mind about doing the right thing for Ohio notwithstanding that new taxes, even temporary taxes, meant great political jeopardy for you. Even though the national economy curtailed your plans for the last term, I'm thankful that you were at the helm.

The occasion that stands out most in my mind, though, happened at the Fair. I was making one of my daily trips to your trailer when you asked me to ride around the fair grounds with you. As we were riding around in your golf cart and the fairgoers were waving and cheering you, you noticed a small girl in the crowd with her mother. It was obvious from their appearance that the day at the Fair was a very special thing for them and was not easily affordable. You had Danny and Bob put them with us in your golf cart and then we stopped at what seemed every concession stand to be sure they had everything they wanted. I cherish that occasion for it was the day that I understood what drove you to public service. It was valuable insight.

Before ending, I want to remind you of what was the most humorous moment during my years with you, and there were many from which to choose. We were talking about a school issue with Vern, Myrl, Oliver and Frank Walter in your office. You had just come back from a speech in southern Ohio and had stopped along the way to buy vegetables to make soup, gallons of soup.

As the school issue was being discussed, Frank was husking corn, Myrl was slicing tomatoes, Vern was in the kitchen stirring the vegetables together, and Oliver was in the vibrating chair exclaiming that it was a 'mell of a hess!' I was talking to Mrs. Rhodes on the phone to find out how to make vegetable soup. I think she had the best laugh of all!

As they say, 'those were the days!'

Lain, Macy, Clinton and I enclose our best wishes and thanks,

—Robert Howarth

*R*hodes' love of the office was not based on a desire for power or the honors and perks that went with it. The love was based on his drive to improve the life of the citizens of Ohio. He did not become wealthy from his many years of service in political office, and any wealth that he had was gained after he left the office of governor in 1971.

Alice Widner, a columnist in New York City, visited Rhodes during his second term in office to learn about his efforts to increase the opportunities for youth through expanding vocational education. Before embarking on a tour of some of the vocational facilities, she met with Rhodes. "There is no crap in him," she said with emphasis as she walked out of his office.

Several people need special recognition since they worked very closely with the governor and had an effect on the total operation of his administrations. The first would be Roy Martin, who worked with the governor during all four of his administrations. Martin came from

Portsmouth, Ohio, and served with Rhodes when he was auditor of Ohio and again when he was governor. Roy was responsible for all political appointments while Rhodes was in office and handled any personnel problems.

Roy knew Rhodes' principles and practices and Rhodes knew that Roy would apply the rules with common sense and loyalty. As a result of Roy's competence and commitment, there were during any of Rhodes' administrations few personnel problems that grew into major problems.

There was always a person in the governor's office keeping track of important activities and who could be reached at any hour of the day or night. He advised the governor daily on legislation and the progress of important initiatives. It was the responsibility of this person to determine that no problem blind-sided the governor. The person had to be selfless, as well as capable of keeping track of many things, including the whereabouts of the governor himself.

The first person to have this responsibility was John McElroy, a quiet man who was seldom noticed by the news media but was intelligent and knowledgeable about the operations of government. Never flustered, he worked tirelessly on behalf of the governor and knew when to make decisions himself and when to take them to "the Boss."

The second person to have this responsibility was Thomas Moyer. Moyer, an attorney, served for about two years but was interested in becoming a judge. The governor appointed him and Moyer since has been twice elected the Chief Justice of the Supreme Court of Ohio.

The third person that served in this role was Robert Howarth, who served in this capacity during Rhodes' last two terms. All three were unusual men who kept the wheels of the machine of state well-oiled and maneuvered around major stumbling blocks.

The three persons who advised the governor on the finances of state during his administrations also deserve special recognition. These three helped Governor Rhodes to have probably the finest management of money of any governor during this century, as well as the best relationships with the state legislature, even though the legislature was under the control of the Democratic Party during Rhodes' last two terms.

The first person to hold the position as director of finance was Richard Krabach. Krabach was committed to living within the set budget, capable of assisting the governor to plan the financing of visionary projects, and ruthless in implementing the legislation and policies that would bring about the progress promised. Krabach was the perfect person for the position as the governor took office for his first term. When the governor faced a budget deficit upon first taking office, Krabach suggested trimming employees of state government by ten percent to balance the budget. The reduction was implemented and the budget was balanced. Krabach later became city manager for the city of Cincinnati.

Howard Collier, Richard Krabach's assistant, became the second person to hold the position. The ability to work with the legislature and to work long hours were the hallmarks of his term. He resigned to become the comptroller of the new College of Medicine at the University of Toledo and returned to his former position for a short period of time during Rhodes' third term.

The third person to hold the position was William Wilkins, who carried on the high expectations of the office even though the position was not as demanding as during Rhodes' first two terms. Wilkins is now the director of finance for a large hospital organization in Columbus.

In working with staff or the public, Governor Rhodes always had the common touch. A guileless man, he was as comfortable—and interested—in talking with a day laborer as he was with a head of state or a movie star.

Lou Holtz, the former coach at Notre Dame University, said in his book, *Winning Every Day*, that if you must make a judgement about a person, ask yourself:

*1. Do I trust him?*

If not, why not. Has he ever lied to you? Will he take ethical shortcuts? Does he speak in lawyer-ese, using deliberately vague, misleading, or ambiguous language?

*2. Is he committed to excellence?*

Is this fellow a workhorse or a shirker? Is he the last to arrive at the office and the first to leave? Does he immediately blame others when anything goes awry or does he assume responsibility for mistakes? Compare his work habits with those of his colleagues and see how he stacks up.

*3. Does he care about you?*

Each person will have his own criteria, but generally you can tell if a person really cares about you if they demonstrate respect for your opinions and feelings.

*J*ames A. Rhodes didn't fit under a microscope, and the loyalty and love of the people to whom he gave leadership, the respect that he engendered even from the opposite party, and the concern that he showed for people indicated that he fit Holtz' definition. He demonstrated concern even for members of the opposite party. In 1998, Oliver Ocasek, who had been a leader on the Democratic side of senate for many years during Rhodes' terms of office, became seriously ill with cancer. Even though Rhodes was in a wheelchair, he was driven from Columbus to Akron to visit with former Senator Ocasek and to encourage his fight.

The governor remained visionary, consistent in his efforts, loyal and caring to those with whom he worked, honest and open in his dealings, and committed to the citizens of Ohio.

# The Rhodes' initiatives

When voters go to the polls, every politician knows they "vote their pocketbook." Keeping taxes low and running on the platform of doing so is the way of campaigning for state offices. The Rhodes' campaigns of "No new taxes" were no exception. During his tenure tax rates were increased, however. The alcoholic beverage tax, the cigarette tax, and the motor fuel tax were all increased.

The largest increase in terms of yield was the state sales tax that had been at the three percent rate from 1935 but went up to four percent in 1967 and five percent in 1981 during the Rhodes' years. In 1972, Governor Gilligan promoted the state income tax while Rhodes was out of office. It remained in place during Rhodes' third and fourth terms and continued thereafter. The result on the general revenue fund (GRF) income during the sixteen years of the Rhodes administration was as follows:

⟶ The Governor presses the flesh
while on an industrial visit.

## Ohio general revenue tax receipts—
## The Rhodes years

### (In millions of $)

| First Eight Years | | Second Eight Years | |
|---|---|---|---|
| **F Y** | **Receipts** | **F Y** | **Receipts** |
| 1964 | $ 533.1 | 1976 | $ 2,538.6 |
| 1965 | 529.8 | 1977 | 2,844.5 |
| 1966 | 628.4 | 1978 | 3,366.0 |
| 1967 | 642.9 | 1979 | 3,719.0 |
| 1968 | 822.1 | 1980 | 3,954.4 |
| 1969 | 952.8 | 1981 | 4,331.1 |
| 1970 | 1,085.8 | 1982 | 4,749.9 |
| 1971 | 1,137.4 | 1983 | 5,728.6 |

From beginning to end of the sixteenth year, the operating income of the state budget thus increased in size by the multiple of ten. In each of the eight-year periods, GRF income doubled, which was as much the result of inflation as tax increases. The management problem most severe was one of balancing operating appropriations between public education and public welfare, each of which continuously pressed for more than a third of the total GRF income. The governor was necessarily the "point man" in this biennial face-off.

During the sixteen years both the education and welfare spokespersons grew increasingly critical that their share was not enough for their needs. Rhodes took the heat and spoke his piece when the situation demanded, an unavoidable dialogue for governors wherever and whenever they serve.

## Capital improvements

The two different theories of public capital improvements are best stated as pay-as you-use vs. pay-as-you-build. As a result of his years as mayor, Jim Rhodes was already a convert to the pay-as-you-use method. Before his first term, Ohio had two bond issues, one to pay World War II bonuses and a highway issue for $500 million, passed at the end of the Lausche administration as a legislative initiative without his support.

Rhodes rebuilt Ohio's systems of higher education, parks, highways, airports and government buildings using an innovative and complex system of bond financing (pay-as-you-use) involving changes in the state constitution and appropriation procedures.

During the Rhodes years, particularly the first eight,

five sections of Article VIII of the Ohio Constitution were
implemented as follows:

1. *Capital Improvements Obligations—Article VIII, Section
2e—*General Obligation bonds may be issued for
site acquisition, construction, and improvement of
buildings for correctional institutions, mental health
facilities, state-supported universities and colleges, and
state offices.

2. *Improvements Bonds—Article VIII, Section 2f*
This section authorizes bonds to be issued for site
acquisition, construction, and improvement of
buildings and facilities, excluding highways, for land
acquisition and development for parks and recreation
and conservation of natural resources, and for use in
conjunction with federal grants or loans for similar
purposes.

3. *Highway Improvement Bonds—Article VIII, Section 2g*
This section of the Ohio Constitution provides for the
issuance of general obligation bonds to acquire rights-
of-way and to construct and reconstruct highways.

4. *Development Bonds—Article VIII, Section 2h*
Purposes authorized by this section include site
acquisition and construction of structures for
institutions of higher education and state government,
flood control, parks and recreation sites and highways
within them, assistance to political subdivisions to
finance construction and extension of water and sewer
lines, stream flow improvements, and construction of
airports and historical or education facilities.

*5. Public Improvements Bonds—Article VIII, Section 2i*
Section 2i authorizes the issue of both general
obligation bonds and revenue bonds. General
obligation bonds are intended to create jobs, enhance
employment opportunities, and improve the economic
welfare of the people of the state.

*T*he administrative and legislative implementation
of these constitutional authorities allowed for a
system where the legislature could appropriate
funds for debt service without pledging the full faith
and credit of the state. In other words, tax monies could
be used to support revenue bonding. The legislature
appropriates from ten funds for debt service:

General Revenue Fund;
Public Improvements Fund;
Wildlife Fund;
Parks and recreation Improvement Fund;
Mental Health Facilities Improvement Fund;
Bureau of Employment Services Fund;
Waterways Safety Fund;
Higher Education Improvement Fund;
Federal Special Revenue Fund;
Highway Operating Fund.

And pays debt service from these seven funds:

Public Improvements Bond Retirement Fund;
Development Bond Retirement Fund;
Highway Obligations Construction Fund;

Higher Educational Improvement Fund;
Improvements Fund;
Mental Health Facilities Improvement Fund;
Parks and Recreation Improvement Fund.

Additions included rental payments appropriated to the Ohio Public Facilities Commission and the 1983 addition of the Housing Finance Authority that was authorized at the November 2, 1982, election when Rhodes was leaving office.

The administrative units which managed the ebb and flow of this pay-as-you-use complex included primarily the following:

*1. Commissioner of the Sinking Fund*
The commissioners included the state's governor, auditor and treasurer who were responsible for the issuance of those bonds supported by the full faith and credit of the state and were approved by direct vote of the people.

*2. Ohio Building Authority*
Created by statute as a non-taxable entity, both corporate and politic, with five members to perform governmental functions but not directly pledging the state's full faith and credit. The purpose was to issue bonds to build state buildings, including prisons used by state agencies (and local and federal agencies in some circumstances,) the rent from which use is used to retire the bonds and manage the buildings.

*3. Ohio Public Facilities Commission*
Created primarily to issue bonds supporting higher

education building. Also included were bonds supporting mental health and state park facilities.

*4. Ohio Air Quality Development Authority*
Created in 1970 to issue bonds to pay for pollution control projects for Ohio industries by using tax-exempt revenue bonding for long low-cost capital financing of facilities to be paid down with use payments for the facility during its lifetime. The Authority had seven members including the ex-officio of the Ohio directors of Health and Environmental Protection.

*5. Ohio Water Development Authority*
Created in 1968 to issue bonds to assist local governments and private businesses with clean water and solid waste projects. The Authority has eight members including as ex-officio the directors of Development, Natural Resources, and Environmental Protection. The debt service for the bonds is paid with long-term use payments.

This detailed description of the Ohio system of bond financing is an integral but little-reported part of the Jim Rhodes political history. Twice in his career his efforts to take this system to the voters were defeated at the polls. First, the effort to create a single Ohio Bond Commission to run the system was defeated by partisan opposition in his second term and, second, the 1975 effort to "package" housing, transportation, industrial development and urban assistance bonding also was defeated at the polls by partisan campaigning.

As a consequence and resulting from the Rhodes' practice of always looking for alternatives, the system in place today is primarily the result of legislative action piece by piece. Rhodes achieved his objective through alternate routes. The search for such legislative alternates was easier during the first eight years when the legislative control was with his party, however, after an initial bit of critical sparks from both sides, he worked equally well in his second eight years with the general assembly in Democratic control.

The eight general assemblies, during his sixteen years, were divided by party as follows:

| General Assembly | Years | Senate | House |
|---|---|---|---|
| 104th | 1963–1964 | 20R-13D | 88R-49D |
| 105th | 1965–1966 | 16R-16D | 75R-62D |
| 106th | 1967–1968 | 23R-10D | 62R-37D |
| 107th | 1969–1970 | 21R-12D | 64R-35D |
| 110th | 1975–1976 | 21D-12R | 59D-40R |
| 111th | 1977–1978 | 21D-12R | 62D-37R |
| 112th | 1979–1980 | 18D-15R | 62D-37R |
| 113th | 1981–1982 | 18R-15D | 54D-43R |

# The great communicator

There must be thousands of quotes from the campaign trail, press conferences and "Rhodes Raider" trips. A collection is printed here without any attempt to determine the original report. The reporters most frequently used as resources include Lee Leonard, United Press International; Bob Miller, Associated Press; Brian Usher and Abe Zaidan, *Akron-Beacon Journal*; Steve Wilson, Gannett News Service; Tom Diemer, Rick Zimmerman and Joe Rice, Cleveland *Plain Dealer*.

"The press people are like dogs in heat. If you stand still, you get screwed. If you run away, they chase after you and bite you in the ass."

—*Rhodes giving advice to an unidentified aid*

⌒ The Governor hits the links with Bob Hope
in the 1970s while Hope was performing at the state fair.

"Rhodes plays the press like a fiddle," said Lee Leonard, veteran UPI Statehouse correspondent. "He knows how we're going to handle each story, what will produce headlines, and he knows the value of timing."

Ask Jim Rhodes about his relations with the press and he would say: "There's no use trying to tell a reporter what to write or trying to tell some editor to endorse somebody. You can't do it."

Inevitably, at some point, he added: "I've never been a candidate for editor."

One of his most severe critics was Abe Zaidan of the *Akron Beacon Journal*, the paper's former political editor, who said of Rhodes, "He has a 'sit, whittle, and spit' kind of humor that is perfect for this state. He has a unique way of convincing voters that he is for everything they are for. That way he brings together Democrat and Republican voters under one roof on election day."

One of Rhodes' favorite quips was about Richard Nixon and his relations with the press in the wake of Watergate. "Nixon was out in California on the beach and found he could walk on water," Rhodes said. "After he walked about fifteen feet and came back, he called over the reporters to watch him. He walked out again and the headlines the next day said, *Nixon can't swim.*"

Reporter Rick Zimmerman had been a constant burr in Rhodes' otherwise easy-riding saddle. He revealed that Rhodes had attended OSU for only a single quarter and was on academic probation when he dropped out.

"When you came here you were a reporter for Harry Horvitz's two small newspapers," Rhodes recalled.

"Yes, Governor," Zimmerman replied.

" And you went with the *Dayton Journal Herald* and then became the main Columbus reporter for *The Plain Dealer,* the biggest in Ohio."

"Yes, Governor."

"And now you have a shot at the Washington bureau."

"That's right, Governor."

"Zimmerman," Rhodes mused with a wry grin, "you've come a long way on my ass."

Former *Boston Journal* writer Abe Zaidan once described his close encounters with Rhodes this way: "An interview with James Allen Rhodes is like trying to tow a lumbering old barge into harbor on the end of a kite string. "You are usually left holding only the string."

" *R*hodes is the Casey Stengel of the gubernatorial fraternity," national columnist Jules Witcover once wrote, likening the governor's verbal goulash to that of the immortal New York Yankee manager.

*On his love for Ohio sports*:
"Woody Hayes once introduced me as the biggest athletic supporter in the state of Ohio."

*On his popularity in the Republican Party*:
"The Democrats said I wasn't fit to sleep with hogs. The Republicans defended me and said I was."

*On George Voinovich, who served as Rhodes' lieutenant governor before he ran for mayor of Cleveland*:
"George was the greatest lieutenant governor in the history of Ohio. He got out in six months and never bothered anybody. The other lieutenant governors were always checking with my doctor about my health every six months."

*On cuisine in his home in Jackson County*:
"Jackson is the Shaker Heights of Appalachia. A seven course dinner down there is a possum and a six pack."

*On wealth*:
"The best way to get rich is to use other peoples' money," Rhodes advised traveling reporters on how they could make money on their salaries.

*On thievery*:
"If you permit a person to steal and you profit from

it, you must take him home each night, coddle him, and watch him day and night. So stop it at the beginning."

"Any schoolboy knows that Akron has the worst downtown in Ohio. I was in downtown Akron recently and had to kill three snakes just to get to the First National Tower," Rhodes said in a private meeting with Akron leaders on why they should support his 1975 bonding proposal.

"When I talk about this, I ain't E. F. Hutton—nobody listens," Rhodes complained to a newspaper editor about having trouble selling his ideas on solving the natural gas crisis of 1977.

"I'm not one of those people that likes to take my Bible and say it's the Republican platform," he said. "I'm for the people. As governor, we didn't follow every elephant that goes by. You can't follow every donkey either. You get too close to 'em and you smell like 'em."

"I was in business and successful and needed to be governor again like I needed a hole in my head. But they kept after me. Everything that happened I would get a dissertation from Gilligan on how bad I was as governor as the reason I couldn't run again," Rhodes said in an interview on why he launched his comeback campaign for governor.

"Concession is good for the soul," Rhodes said to perplexed aides who wondered why he had made the "early concession" speech to John Gilligan on election night of 1974 after two networks incorrectly declared him the loser in the governor's race.

"Ohio is a big state. You have to run and lose first. I never had any objection to being a loser," Rhodes said

Governor Rhodes in Israel
in the 1960s with Golda Meier.

during an 1982 interview on the lesson he learned by losing to Frank Lausche in the governor's race.

On the rejection of his $4.5 billion bond issue by voters in 1975, he said, "It's not what you accomplish. It's what you put before the people. We have no failures. We're talking about 500,000 people out of a job. Not me, I have a job. We've had no setbacks. We'll have programs. We've always had programs."

He gave this advice to governor-elect Richard Celeste: "The only two jobs where you start on top are digging a hole and governor."

Ducking a question on whether he would run for the U.S. Senate in 1982, he said, "I'm not considering anything and I know it's difficult to say that."

When it was pointed out he had not answered yes or no, he said, "I don't generally answer yes or no."

Joking to a predominately Jewish crowd at a black tie celebration of Israel's thirtieth anniversary: "Once I was staying at a hotel in Tel Aviv and the housekeeper kept asking me, 'What was your name before you changed it?' Finally, the tenth time she asked me that, I told her, 'Rhodes-enberg.' "

"I got the nomination to run against Lausche in 1954 when I was out of town," Rhodes said. "I knew nothing about it. I had no business running against Lausche." Apparently, he was right. He faced Democrat Frank Lausche and for the second time was denied the governor's office. Later, when asked whom he most admired in politics, he named Frank Lausche as "the best person in public life."

"Lausche was gifted," Rhodes said. "Lausche could answer a question in such a way that there were three sides to it. Everybody was satisfied."

Asked if he had learned his similar talent from Lausche, Rhodes said, "I was never that good. I wished I was."

" *I*t's all in the timing. You don't bash a rabbit the first time he sticks his head out of a hole. Ignore him awhile and let him get away from it," Rhodes said to aides during a discussion of when to respond to attacks by candidate Richard Celeste in the 1978 race.

Rhodes often said he never got mad or stayed mad at anybody. "You can't get so mad at somebody one day that you can't reach a compromise the next morning."

*Chapter nine*

"Legislators will often tear me apart during a floor session," he said, "and the next week they're down here wanting their picture taken because of some bill. We take the picture."

He said the secret to success was what the Indians' pitcher, Satchel Paige, said: "Don't look back. Somebody may be gaining on you."

Asked what he wanted to be remembered for, he said instantly, "Nothing. Why should anyone push anything upon themselves? Ten years from now they'll look at that same statue and say, 'When was he governor?'"


*D*rink up, he told Ohioans in 1965—tomato juice, that is.

"If every Ohioan would drink an extra sixteen ounce can of tomato juice a year, 2,000 jobs would be created in Ohio," he said. That would mean $13 million more in personal income, enough to support 6,240 persons, pay the rent on 2,320 homes, and educate 1,020 children, Rhodes figured. To get the program rolling, Rhodes installed a merry-go-round in the Statehouse rotunda and loaded it with tomato juice cans.

On economic development, he said, "Jobs, jobs, jobs."

*On losing elections*: "The people have spoken. I will abide by their decision."

*On private industry*: "Profit is not a dirty word in Ohio."

*On the environment*: "Blaming Ohio for acid rain is like blaming Florida for hurricanes."

*On his strong support of cancer research*: "If you live long enough and your heart stays good, cancer will eventually kill you."

*On candidates who wanted his job as governor*: "If they want to be governor, let them run. Let them all run. We have no objections."

*On politicians*: "One election doesn't make a career."

*On Ohio*: "Ohio has more things by accident than most states have on purpose."

*On Ohioans*: "The average Ohioans wants a job and wants to be left alone."

*On leadership*: "You can do one of three things. Lead, follow, or get out of the way."

*I*t was the ultimate Rhodes Raiders trade mission on that hot July day in 1979. Six months after the U.S. officially recognized China, Rhodes was in Peking trying to make capitalists out of Communists. He told them they should build a Disney World at the Peking Airport and an escalator up the Great Wall of China. Ever since he sponsored turtle races at his campus restaurant in the 1930's near Ohio State, Rhodes had been the master of perpetual promotions.

He went to the National Governors Conference held

on the U.S.S. Independence off the coast of the Virgin Islands. "They asked me which room I wanted," recalled Rhodes. "I said, 'Where's Rocky (New York govenor Nelson Rockefeller)?'

"They said, 'Why?'

"I said, 'because if that ship sinks, I know they're gonna come after *him*."

*R*hodes was in Peking in 1979 on a trade mission. He met with a group of Chinese government officials. "Ohio is No.1 in rubber, No.1 in glass, No. 1 in machine tools, No.1 in auto parts!" exclaimed Rhodes, waving his index finger under the nose of his host, Xiao Fan, vice chairman of the Chinese Council for the Promotion of International trade.

Rhodes bragged about the exploits of Ohio born aviators and astronauts. "Wright brothers!" he croaked and flapped his arms at Xiao.

Then he pulled out a dollar bill and told his hosts, "We're here to make China green."

As governor, Rhodes was always under fire by the environmentalists about acid rain caused by smoke-belching Ohio industries. He liked to tell the story about the little boy ordered by his mother to eat his Wheaties— that there were 200 million starving Chinese children who would like to be able to eat the cereal.

"Name one," said the boy.

"We're like the boy," Rhodes would say. "People say 51,000 people have been killed by acid rain. Name one."

Rhodes was accosted on the campaign trail in northwestern Ohio by a lady who was berating him for something he hadn't done.

"Why, that's a legislative problem," said Rhodes. "You should talk to your legislators about that.

"Then he spied *Akron Beacon Journal* reporter Mike Cull. "Here's Senator Cull," Rhodes said. "He'll help you out."

"I'm not a senator," protested Cull.

"Now don't try to get out of it," said Rhodes, and left the helpless Cull in the clutches of the irate woman.

Rhodes was good at ducking and diving when it came to dealing with the news media. Reporters lived for the day when they could catch him. UPI's Lee Leonard was sure he had Rhodes cornered one day during a campaign when Rhodes was blasting away at government bureaucrats who couldn't get a job in the private sector.

"Governor, you have been in government for thirty-six years and only in the private sector for four years," Leonard said.

"Yes," Rhodes retorted, "and did forty years of work."

*R*hodes refused to take part in the traditional City Club Forum debate with Celeste a few days before the 1978 election. After his victory, Rhodes cracked, "Celeste debated an empty chair and the chair won."

Reporters who covered Rhodes were familiar with his somewhat peculiar eating habits. Ed Heinke remembered an incident at the governor's conference in Denver attended by the governor and his wife.

Mrs. Rhodes wanted to go to a fancy restaurant and got dressed up. Rhodes got a limousine and off they went. But on the way to the restaurant, Rhodes had the driver stop at a supermarket where he bought a hunk of bologna and a loaf of bread, and the governor and his wife had dinner in the car.

That was the governor's idea of a satisfying dinner.

*R*hodes was extolling Ohio's tourist attractions. "What we have here in the way of parks and recreation and other facilities for people to stay over night—when you go to any other state or surrounding states or the Tetons or any of the national lodges that they have—they're all tool sheds. We're the only place that they have an indoor swimming pool outdoors."

And how did Rhodes know about Ohio's tourist attractions? "I am the only governor in the history of Ohio who has visited every museum, every cultural center, every fair, every park, and every attraction that we have in the state of Ohio. I am the only governor who has visited every ski lodge—and every ski and snowmobile in the state of Ohio."

One cold winter, Governor Rhodes ordered the PUCO to make sure utilities kept the heat turned on for poor people and worry about receiving payment later.

Reporters asked him, "What if they don't pay their bills all winter? Aren't you inviting them to not pay their bills?"

"They might want air conditioning," Rhodes quickly responded.

Friend and foe alike were in awe of Rhodes' unique political abilities. Paul Tipps, former Democratic State Chairman, said of Rhodes, "Damn, I wish we could clone him. Whether you agree with him or not, you must respect his political acumen and his ability to communicate with people. I have nothing but respect for him. Fortunately, he is one of a kind for Republicans."

*W*hen leaving office in 1970, Rhodes, his voice nearly breaking, told the legislators, "There is a certain spiritual satisfaction that comes to a man of humble origin whom destiny has given the opportunity to lead millions of his fellow men. When one leaves such a position, he is hopeful that he has kept the faith and trust that was placed in him by so many."

One long-time friend recalled a conversation in Rhodes' office where a man was complaining bitterly because one of the governor's lieutenants, Roy Martin, had failed to make an appointment with someone the GOP county chairman thought was important.

"He was just raising hell about it and Rhodes was saying, "Yes, yes, yes."

"After he left, I asked him, 'If Roy's causing you problems, why don't you change him?'"

Rhodes said, "Never take the punching bag out of the gym."

The translation, according to Rhodes, was: "If someone else is taking the heat, you don't have to."

A *Plain Dealer* reporter was talking with Rhodes about a series of articles reporting the worsening of lakes and streams in New York, New England, and parts of Canada, believed to be caused by acid rain from Ohio.

"Listen," the governor said. "Ohio's miners have to work and Ohio people don't want big utility bills."

"Yes, Governor," someone asked, "but what about all those frogs and fish you're killing in New York?"

"Frogs and feesh ('fish' in Rhodes' language) don't vote in Ohio," he said. "Maybe they vote in New York, but not in Ohio."

"Ohio is in trouble tonight," he said at the peak of the 1978 blizzard. In the same statement, what sounded like a canned quote popped out: "It's a killer blizzard looking for victims."

Ohioans stranded in their homes saw on television a governor genuinely touched by their plight and doing all he could to help. Some thought they saw a tear in his eye. Critics charged that Rhodes capitalized on a crises, even overstating its seriousness.

The next time it snowed one of the skeptics sniffed, "It's a killer flurry looking for victims."

"*H*e was reading in a little country newspaper about this flood," his then-executive assistant Thomas Moyer recalled. "He saw a quote by the mayor of this little town, a woman. She said, "Nobody cares about us down here. We're not going to get any help.' The governor said, 'We're going down there.'"

Within hours, Rhodes was in a plane headed for a remote hamlet in Belmont County with the unlikely name of Goosetown. He brought the Statehouse press corps along. What they saw was a community paralyzed and isolated by floodwaters of the Little Wheeling Creek that had frozen solid.

"We're here to help," Rhodes declared.

"That to me was the essence of the man," Moyer said, "He understood what it means to suffer and have the feeling that nobody cares."

Upon learning that seventy-nine of his gubernatorial papers had been taken to a Columbus dump by mistake and buried, he said, "That was all correspondence and there was nothing in that of any consequence—letters between congressmen and the legislature and all that. They've been keeping papers for a hundred years at the historical society and I don't think they've had one request from anybody to look at them."

The metaphor that best suited Rhodes was supplied by George Forbes, the autocratic president of the Cleveland City Council, who said, "Rhodes is a master juggler. He keeps twenty balls going in the air and you never know which to keep your eye on. There's no question he's the best politician I ever met—just keeping all those balls in the air."

Said Peter O'Grady when he was running Gilligan's campaign, "Jim was probably the cleverest politician I've ever had the opportunity to campaign against. He's slippery. He's elusive. He was eighteen points behind Gilligan after the primary. There's no way in the world he should have won the race. We handed it to them. He snuck in the back door."

"Be like the camel," Rhodes said. "Get your head in the tent." Rhodes says that he "sat in the catbird seat ten years (as state auditor). We knew where the bodies were buried. We knew the people who were working. We knew the people who were not. We knew every facet of the operation" as the result of a "ten-year course in state government." It was helpful, he says, because "it's difficult to come in here off the street and run the state."

When Rhodes first entered the governor's office in 1963, he found the carpet gone, no telephone service, and the plumbing shut down. It was sort of a parting shot by the man Rhodes had beaten in the general election two months earlier, Democrat Michael DiSalle.

"Being governor is a full time job," Rhodes said. "The governor sets the pace. If I'm here at 7:30, everybody's here at 7:30. If I am here at 8, it's 8. If I don't work, nobody else wants to work."

On July 7, 1965, Govenor James A. Rhodes, never one to think small, proposed building a bridge from Ohio to Canada. Rhodes proposed either one from Cleveland, which would connect with Port Stanley, Ontario, or one from Sandusky, which would go to Point Pelee. Rhodes said the bridge would be an economic boon to Ohio and Canada. "We are well beyond the age when this would be considered a wild idea," he said.

The date was September 12, 1976, and Bill Cohen, Statehouse reporter for Ohio Public Radio, had this interview when Rhodes was addressing a conference of lobbyists.

**Rhodes:** "You don't want to go home and say: 'What did he say and where does he stand?' We're here to answer questions and this is part of the business. If you can't answer them, get out of the business."

**Cohen:** "Governor, are you in favor of the mandatory seat belt law?"

**Rhodes:** "I haven't even given it any thought. I thought it was the law."

**Cohen:** "It is. Do you favor it or not?"

**Rhodes:** "I don't know. I put on a seat belt every time. I'm following the law."

**Cohen:** "Do you think it should be the law?"

**Rhodes:** "I don't know. I haven't asked anybody.

I haven't heard any appraising of it, and I haven't seen any polls."

**Cohen:** "Some people want to repeal the seat belt law. Do you think that's a good idea?"

**Rhodes:** "Put it on the ballot."

**Cohen:** "You told the crowd here, 'If you can't answer the questions, get out of the business.' Let me try one more time. Are you for the seat belt law or are you against it?"

**Rhodes:** "Let me say…I'll explain it to you for the fifth time. It's the law on the books. As the governor, I have to enforce the law. If they want it changed they have to go to the secretary of state to get a ballot that complies with the state statute, get the signatures, and come back to the secretary of state and put it on the ballot. Then I'll tell you what happens."

In an interview on national politics at the end of his record sixteen years as governor, he said, "I never had a great desire to go to Washington. The glory road never did anything for my ego.…"


*J*im Rhodes was comfortable with persons in any walk of life. He had lived and survived at both ends of the economic spectrum. He respected people who did their job regardless of their wealth or lack thereof. He respected but was not overawed by individuals with wealth and power.

One of his favorite politicians was Nelson Rockefeller. The Rhodes-Rockefeller relationship went back to 1962 when they met at West Virginia's Greenbriar resort. "Rhodes impressed Rocky because Rhodes was such a free spirit," said one insider who observed the relation-

Governor Rhodes in Cleveland supporting
Nelson Rockefeller in his bid for the Presidency.

ship first hand. "It's like the rich kid getting infatuated
with the poor kid across the tracks. Rhodes talked up to
Rocky, and he liked it."

On one occasion, several Rocky aides recalled, Rockefeller asked Rhodes advice on divorcing his wife and
marrying Happy, his second wife. "It's bad politics,"
Rhodes advised him: "Rocky, if I had your money, I'd
build a castle, fill it with naked women and sit around
with a whip."

Truman once stated that Rhodes was his favorite governor, and Democrat Lyndon B. Johnson, in 1967, called
Rhodes "one of my best friends" and gave him a person-
ally guided tour of the White House. Why? Rhodes was
a staunch defender of Johnson's Vietnam Policy. When
opposition arose in congress in 1966, Rhodes pushed

through the National Governor's Conference a resolution backing Johnson's policy. It won unanimous approval.

When Governor Ronald Reagan returned from the 1968 Republican National Convention, Richard Nixon had won the GOP nomination for president. Reagan returned to California a loser, but he offered a startling revelation to the California press corps: If he had been nominated, Reagan would have asked Ohio Governor James Rhodes to be his vice presidential running mate.

"Frankly, in my mind," he said, "Jim Rhodes is as good a man as we could have. I had no second choice."

# *Political flak*

Participating in the political process guarantees the office-holder political bombs or flak, for decisions real or imagined. James Rhodes faced his share of these, but he was never proved to have acted dishonestly in seeking or functioning in a public office.

### Campaign funds

During the first campaign for the office of governor, against DiSalle, DiSalle dropped a bombshell late in the campaign, accusing Rhodes of converting $54,000 of his campaign funds to personal use. Rhodes owned up to it, but said he'd already paid back the money and satisfied the IRS. This was one of only two attacks that Rhodes ever answered. It was obvious the DiSalle information was "bootlegged" from Washington, D.C.

The *Akron Beacon Journal* was given credit for "feeding" the story. The newspaper story was that Rhodes had tapped his Rhodes for Auditor and Rhodes Volunteer Committee treasuries for at least $54,982. The *Beacon Journal* reported that he used the money for

Rhodes sworn in for third
term, 1975, by Judge Frank Celebresse.

personal expenses—not for political purposes—including payments on a new home, a new car, and to pay his federal income tax.

The IRS audit showed Rhodes had reported voluntarily that he converted $18,982 of the $54,982 to his personal use. There was no law against using campaign funds for personal use, as long as it was reported as income. The incident involved no public funds or law breaking.

According to the *Beacon Journal* and DiSalle, Rhodes also received $36,000 in what he termed "loans" from the Rhodes for Auditor Fund from July 22,1954, through December 11, 1957, also not illegal.

Rhodes used $5,500 for his home in Columbus. He paid another $4,000 to an Oldsmobile dealer. He used

$12,000 to pay federal income taxes in 1956 and 1957. He used the rest—$15,000—for "miscellaneous expenses" during the four years. Although Rhodes told the IRS these were loans from his campaign fund, he had never paid them back.

So in 1958, the IRS required Rhodes to pay back taxes on the $36,000 or to repay the loans with interest of $3,072. He chose to repay the loans in July and August of 1958, according to federal sources. That was the end of that story for everyone except the press.

## The *Life* magazine bomb

The most authoritative account of this political buncombe is from the legal mind of Louis Nizer who wrote of the incident in his 1978 legal memoir, *Reflections Without Mirrors* (Doubleday & Company, Inc. Garden City, New York). The incident involved *Life* magazine and the 1970 campaign.

The chief accusation, Nizer reported, was that Governor Rhodes had commuted Thomas (Yonnie) Licavoli's life sentence for murder in the first degree to second degree. This turned out to be on the unanimous recommendation of the parole board, whose decision the governor accepted. This made Licavoli eligible to apply for parole. The article, however, did not reveal this. The subheading in the article gave the flavor of the charge: "Plenty of Money Floating Around to Set Yonnie Free."

The innuendo was unmistakable. There were references to $250,000 being available to free Licavoli and that in the past there had been overtures to previous officials to free Licavoli. They had rejected the proposed bribes, although there was a vacuum in the article as to why they had not reported the matter to criminal authorities. The clear implication was that Rhodes had yielded to temptation.

*Life* magazine was so proud of itself that it took full page advertisements in various newspapers announcing its scoop. One such advertisement appeared in the *New York Times*. Nine-tenths of the page was a huge photograph of Governor Rhodes. Underneath was a large headline: "Ohio's Governor and the Mob."

There was a subtle change from singular to plural. The *Life* article referred to 'mobster.' The *Times'* advertisement referred to 'mob.' The accusation, like the amoeba, had multiplied itself in the course of transition.

"To top it off," said the rest of the ad, "*Life* presents evidence showing that while in public office, Governor Rhodes has engaged in high-handed manipulation of political funds."

"The multiplication of falsehoods created a picture of a vile, unscrupulous hypocrite," wrote Nizer. "Our indignation rose at the outrageous attacks. Who could be safe, if such tactics succeeded? But once again we asked the governor to satisfy us, as counsel, by documentary proof. His accounts forwarded a cent-by-cent analysis refuting every accusation. We advised Governor Rhodes to issue a public statement, setting forth the assets of his wife and family. He did so in detail. After more than twenty years of public service he wound up virtually impoverished. His reward had been the honor of high office and the regard of the people for him. Now even these were taken away (pages 165–166).

"As counsel met to arrange the legal duels on the field of honor, the possibility of ending the lawsuit arose. Would *Life* in writing remove the taint on Governor

Rhodes' integrity? We stated that, aside from the legal problems, damages were not our goal. The restoration of Governor Rhodes' good name was. If this could be achieved we would forego our determination to take the matter, if necessary, to the highest court to review the restrictive rule that made public officials open targets for published lies.

"The editors were decent men and may have regretted the excesses of the publication. An arrangement was concluded. It protected *Life* against humiliation of open confession of misdeed and protected Governor Rhodes by withdrawing the charge of innuendo that he had any association with 'the mob' or had been bribed or influenced improperly in his conduct (page 167)."

By agreement, Governor Rhodes then issued a press release so stating these points. This ended the issue for all but the antagonistic press. The loss of the 1970 primary to Robert Taft was less the result of the *Life* magazine bomb than the tragedy of the Kent State University confrontation between National Guard and the war-protesting young.

Louis Nizer was a best selling author as well as a brilliant lawyer. In addition to *Reflections Without Mirrors* his authorship included *The Jury Returns* and *My Life in Court*. His autograph to James A. Rhodes of his 1968 book where Jim's experience with the *Life* magazine is replayed says, "To Gov. James A. Rhodes, with high regard and admiration."

The issue came up in the campaigns of 1974, 1978, and 1986, without any of the reports making it clear that *Life* had lied by inference and admitted it. As Nizer concluded: "The litigation was withdrawn without prejudice to Governor Rhodes. Later, the real verdict was given by the citizens of Ohio. They elected Rhodes to be governor again. *Life* magazine suspended weekly publication soon after."

## Flap about making money

The history of Rhodes as a private businessman always begins for the critical press in 1970. That year, Rhodes had disclosed his 1969 income—mostly his $40,000 salary as governor—and his stated net worth at the time as $65,000, including $25,000 paid into the Public Employees Retirement System.

In an accompanying statement he said: "I have not been governor for personal profit. I have not made investments of any kind for financial advancement. I own no corporate stock. I own no mutual funds. I own no real estate—not even a home. (He then lived in the governor's mansion.) I am not a director of any company or corporation. I am not a trustee of any fund or the beneficiary of any trust or foundation. I am not a partner in any business enterprise. I have not had nor do I now have, any conflict of interest."

Within two years most of the statements about corporate stock, trusts, partnerships, real estate, and investments were no longer operative. After leaving the office Rhodes set up two development firms: James A. Rhodes and Associates (JAR) with Fred Neuenschwander, his state development director of the 1960s, and he launched H. and R. Development Company. The H was for Don M. Hilliker and the R. was for Rhodes. The partnership with Hilliker was the major reason for Rhodes' present affluence.

Hilliker was a Bellefontaine developer who had

been Rhodes' campaign treasurer in 1966. Rhodes had appointed him to the Ohio Development Finance Commission and The Ohio State University Board of Trustees.

*H*illiker had purchased seven acres of land for $962,000 in 1970 in an area just south of Orlando, Florida, where Walt Disney World was under construction. Hilliker purchased the land from R.F. Raidle of Orlando. Raidle's dream was to develop 3,000 acres at the intersection of the Florida Turnpike and Interstate 4. Raidle, with Walt Disney for a neighbor, was billing his $500 million proposed project as the "biggest construction boom in U.S. history."

In May 1971, Raidle hired JAR and Associates of Columbus to be a development consultant for his project. The project would contain shopping centers, hotels, motels, condominiums, and other commercial and light industrial projects.

Rhodes and Hilliker became heavy investors in the Florida project. H and R. Development built a Howard Johnson's high-rise hotel there in 1971 and a second in 1972 along Interstate 4. In 1973, H. & R. Development Company formed a partnership with Nationwide Insurance, called Buckeye O'Hare Corporation, and built a seven-story $8.1 million hotel at O'Hare International at Chicago. Also in 1973, H. & R. with Huntington National Bank, Columbus, built another hotel and restaurant near Atlanta International Airport.

The first public notice of his role as a stockholder in Wendy's International came with Rhodes financial disclosure statement in 1975 when he disclosed he had

Working on transportation proposal;
development director Fred Neuenschwander
at left, beside the Governor.

some stock received in exchange for consulting work at
JAR & Associates. Later (April 1975), with a loan from a
Cleveland businessman, Harold C. Schott, he purchased
at about $16 a share some $500,000 in Wendy's stock
before it was publicly traded. The stock doubled.

Hilliker and Rhodes, through H. & R. Development
Company, acquired the franchise rights in 1975 to build
and operate forty-eight Wendy's restaurants on Long
Island, forty-eight in New Jersey and twenty in thirteen
counties in Upstate New York, according to records at
the U.S. Securities and Exchange Commission (SEC) in
Washington, D.C. Hilliker was elected to the board of
directors of Wendy's International in April 1976. Wendy's
also assigned H&R franchise rights in Long Island

and New Jersey, according to SEC reports. Then H&R assigned its interest in Upstate New York franchises to Wendeast Corp. for development of restaurants around Albany, N. Y.

On October 4,1986, during the gubernatorial campaign, Rhodes had his certified public accountant, E. C. Redman, reveal his federal income tax returns for the calendar years 1981 through 1985. This record revealed a gross long-term capital gain of $7,150,763 for the five-year period from H&R Development Co. activities (a loss of $127,723 on sale of Wendy stock). At the time (December 31, 1985) James and Helen Rhodes in trust held $3,819,230 in securities not subject to federal income tax (tax exempts), a normal estate management movement of capital at Rhodes' age of 76 at the time. There have been no public reports of his estate since that November 1986 date.

Thus, in retrospective analysis, it is obvious that the mass media could have and should have known the source and extent of the "facts" of Rhodes' moneymaking activities. He was and is a successful developer where "profit is not a dirty word."

The innuendo that his later affluence was the result of illegal, immoral, or political chicanery is untrue and failed to report that he was as successful in business as he was in politics.

# Unprecedented growth

More money was invested in higher
education during the Rhodes' administrations
than was expended in the previous 160 years of
the state's history, and perhaps the longest lasting
improvement made by Rhodes in Ohio was in the
area of education. In his four terms of office there
was a remarkable expansion in which the number of
institutions of higher education increased greatly, the
physical facilities improved vastly, and the operating
support system increased significantly.

Prior to Rhodes, coordination of higher education
among the six state universities was voluntary, and
each university could approach the legislature with its
needs. There were no controls over the proliferation of
degree-granting programs. Under Rhodes' leadership,
coordination of higher education was made a matter of
law, but the management of individual institutions was
not only maintained but also strengthened.

Even as the first eight years of his administration

The Governor making
a speech in the late 1960s.

ended, a new and permanent arrangement for financing capital improvements had been put into place. The period was truly a golden age for higher education in Ohio.

During Rhodes' first eight years, 1963 through 1971, the enrollment in state sponsored and state assisted institutions grew from 90,000 to nearly 280,000 students.

When Rhodes took office, there were only six autonomous state universities. There was a coordinating council for the universities, but the coordinating council did little to coordinate the fiscal requests of the universities into any pattern that considered the needs of all. This coordinating council, known as the Inter-University Council of Ohio, had a representative from each institution. The representation included the president, a trustee, and the business officer of each institution. This council negotiated with the director of finance, the governor, the operating appropriations committees of the legislature, and had an important role in the adoption and implementation of the bond issue endorsed by Governor Lausche in 1955.

*T*he resulting capital improvements had helped the state universities to meet the accumulated plant needs of the 1950s but did nothing to meet the expansion needs of the 1960s. The Inter-University Council had taken one important step late in the 1950s, when it began a cooperative study to determine the cost of instruction by major academic programs and by levels of study (baccalaureate, masters, doctors, and professional). The study was initiated under a consultant and continued under the direction of a full-time director hired by the council and housed at The Ohio State University.

The Inter-University Council could act only by unanimous agreement among the six institutions. In 1961, a serious split developed within the council members on the issue of expanding doctoral degree programs and on the issue of responding to a legislative call for additional capital improvements.

As a result, the council was in considerable disarray as of 1962. During the 1962 campaign, Rhodes issued a statement entitled "The Blueprint for Brainpower." In this statement, Rhodes stated, "It is a matter of urgent economic and cultural importance for Ohio to advance and improve the public structure of higher education." He also advocated the creation of a state board of regents to guide the necessary developments.

The day after his election, November 8, 1962, Rhodes called the university presidents together and told them his plan, much to the chagrin of the group. In January 1963, the Ohio Legislative Service Commission issued a report entitled "Coordination of Higher Education." The report was quite critical of the University Council, citing particularly the development of doctoral degree programs at Ohio University, Kent State University, and Bowling Green University. The report further pointed out that neither the O'Neill Commission of 1959 nor the interim commission of 1959 to 1964 had any authority to do more than make studies and nothing had been accomplished other than the two-year campus legislation of 1961.

The need for a powerful coordinating agency was presented in terms of meeting the unprecedented enrollment growth that would occur during the 1960s. In March 1963, House Bill 214 was introduced. The proposed legislation created an Ohio Board of Regents with nine members and nine-year terms, as a strong coordinating agency for higher education. The legislation was drafted, at the request of Governor Rhodes by a prominent Columbus attorney who had been a trustee of The Ohio State University.

It was clearly evident the measure had the backing of Governor Rhodes and had been designed to carry out his campaign pledge. The provisions of the legislation appeared to be drawn in considerable part from the legislation authorized in the Illinois Board of Higher Education. The designation of "The Board of Regents" originated with Rhodes himself.

The state university presidents and their boards were confronted with a major dilemma when the legislation was introduced. With one exception, the presidents were opposed to the creation of a board of regents. Governor Rhodes had anticipated the opposition and had defused it at the first election meeting. At that meeting, the governor announced that he was prepared to ask the general assembly and the voters of Ohio to pass a $250 million dollar bond issue, of which $175 million would be earmarked for capital improvements for higher education.

This news was indeed welcome to the presidents, who had gone through the years of the DiSalle administration without any capital improvement funds. The message from the governor was loud and clear. First the governor implied that he would not look to the Inter-university Council for any advice on how to spend the capital improvement funds. Second, although no threat of any kind was made or even hinted, it appeared evident that unless a board of regents was created the governor might very well decide not to push for the bond issue.

An informal meeting was held in the speaker's office to discuss the proposed measure for a coordinating board, and the six presidents were cautious in stating their position. They indicated they did not desire to appear in a public hearing to endorse or oppose the legislation for a board of regents. The presidents expressed concern about how a new board of regents might operate, but they also pledged their cooperation with the board, if the general assembly saw fit to enact the legislation.

No action was taken by any of the presidents to organize any opposition to the legislation. If the price of a sizeable and unprecedented program of higher education building was to be the acceptance of a "board of regents," the sacrifice had to be made. Rhodes had correctly assessed the mood of the university presidents and their governing boards. The board of regents was given full and major kinds of authority. The first provision was to make studies for desirable policies for higher education and to formulate a master plan for the development.

The master plan and the modifications from time to time were to be recommendations for action to the governor and the general assembly. Second, the board was authorized to recommend to the governor and the general assembly current operating appropriations and capitol improvement appropriations. Third, the board was given the power to approve any new degree programs to be undertaken by any public institution of higher education. In the fourth place, the board had the power to approve any new campuses to be established for a public institution.

The board of regents succeeded to the authority invested in 1961 in a state community college board. The Ohio Board of Regents did not supercede any of the university boards of trustees. These boards, however, could no longer authorize new degree programs or new branch campuses without the prior approval of the Ohio Board of Regents. The budgeting power, authorized in the past by the University Council, was now formally invested in the Ohio Board of Regents. The management authority of the boards of the individual universities was not diminished by the creation of a new state board. In fact, this management authority was enhanced with new legislation.

In 1963, there were five state universities and one

state college (Central State, which had its designation changed to 'University' in 1965). Only Ohio State was located in a major urban area, and that in the third largest metropolitan center in Ohio. Ohio University, Miami University, Bowling Green University, and Kent State University were located in relatively small communities in the four corners of the state.

Three of these universities were only a few miles from major urban centers, but they were not located in them. There were three municipal universities in Akron, Cincinnati, and Toledo that received no state assistance. There were two community colleges in Cuyahoga County, but they did not begin to receive any state assistance until July 1, 1963. Only two technical institutes had been initiated by the Division of Vocational Education in the State Department of Education.

*I*n the advocacy of the 1963 bond issue, Governor Rhodes insisted that capital improvement funds should be extended to include the municipal university, the community colleges, and the university branches. This decision recognized the population and the voting importance of the urban areas of the state. Ohio was fortunate in not having one large and dominant city. Rather, it had eight prominent urban areas (Cleveland, Cincinnati, Columbus, Toledo, Akron, Dayton, Youngstown, and Canton, all over 100,000 population). It was evident in terms of service and of political reality that greater attention had to be paid in higher education to the large and smaller urban areas of Ohio.

In a special session of the general assembly in

December of 1964, legislation was enacted to establish Cleveland State University and the Medical College of Ohio at Toledo. Cleveland State University was built upon the foundation of Fenn College, a YMCA-sponsored institution. In 1967, legislation was enacted enabling the University of Toledo and the University of Akron to become state universities and providing for the transition of the Miami/Ohio State branch campus near Dayton into Wright State University.

Youngstown State University was also created by law in 1967, taking over the private University of Youngstown. Other legislation provided for state subsidy of various programs at the University of Cincinnati, which became fully a state-assisted university in 1977. As of 1971, there were eleven state universities and one state-aided university, which later became a state university.

Governor Rhodes endorsed the recommendation in the first master plan of the Ohio Board of Regents in 1966 that at least a two-year institution of public higher education should be located within commuting distance of the entire population of the state. Commuting distance was defined as thirty-five miles. By 1971, this objective was achieved for all but about four percent of the state's population.

Of special note was the growth of medical education facilities over the state under the Rhodes administrations. Rhodes was very involved in the extension of medical education. As an example, he believed that hospital facilities at The Ohio State University to be inadequate for both the education of physicians and service to patients. He budgeted funds for the construction of a new hospital to replace the old one.

The president of The Ohio State University went to the

legislature to oppose the construction on the basis it was not needed. Governor Rhodes called the president into his office and told him that he was messing with legislation that was important to the University and for the people of Ohio. He suggested the president should resign and gave him a year to do so. The hospital was built and the president resigned within the suggested time.

During the Rhodes' administrations, the following additions were made to the medical education programs supported by the state:

The Medical College of Ohio, Toledo, Ohio;

The Medical College at Wright State University, Dayton, Ohio;

Northeast College of Medicine, serving three universities, Kent, Cleveland State, and Youngstown;

College of Osteopathy at Ohio University, Athens, Ohio;

Medical College at the University of Cincinnati, Cincinnati, Ohio (formerly supported as a city college).

Two programs that were not in state universities but received state assistance were: The Medical College at Case Western Reserve, Cleveland, Ohio, and The College of Podiatry, Cleveland, Ohio.

## Capital improvements—Rhodes the builder

First win—In November of 1963, the voters of Ohio approved a constitutional amendment authorizing a bond issue of $250 million for capital improvements; $175 million of this total was earmarked for higher education. The appropriation of this bond issue began in the short session of the 1964 general assembly. An appropriation was made to the board of regents to develop a master plan, with emphasis upon the expansion of enrollment and facilities for higher education in Ohio.

Second win—At the special session of the general assembly in December of 1964, Governor Rhodes recommended a second bond issue in the amount of $290 million of which $145 million was to be spent for higher education. The voters of Ohio approved the bond issue at the May 1965 primary. As a result, a total of $320 million had been provided by the Rhodes administration for higher education facilities during the first term of 1963 to 1967. The funds thus made available were appropriated by the general assembly upon recommendation by the governor.

*I*n November of 1966, Governor Rhodes was overwhelmingly re-elected to a second term. A first defeat—By early 1967, the board of regents had developed a capital improvement plan calling for the extensive expansion of the "old" universities, new state universities, community colleges, technical institutes, and university branches. The goal being to meet the labor market demand for educated talent, and the student expectations in Ohio. Governor Rhodes responded to this further recommendation by proposing a third bond issue in 1967.

The recommended constitutional amendment in 1967 was different from those of 1963 and 1965. Instead of a fixed amount of authorized debt, the amendment called for the establishment of an Ohio bond commission to determine capital improvement needs and to sell bonds to meet these needs. In advocating the bond issue, Governor Rhodes asked the state universities to prepare plans for research. This proposal was soundly defeated, with strong opposition from the press.

Early in 1968, Governor Rhodes recommended another bond issue for financing capital facilities. In addition to provisions respecting a continuing program of highway improvements and other capital facilities, the amendments provided for the issuance of revenue bonds by higher education institutions for academic facilities not subject to the debt limitations of the state constitution. In November 1969, the voters at the general election approved the bond issue.

The new legislation provided for the creation of an Ohio public facilities commission that might issue revenue bonds in such amounts and for such projects as the general assembly might authorize. The bonds were to be retired from the pledge of student fees by the institutions of higher education, but the general assembly might reimburse the institutions for the fee income earmarked for capital improvements.

Under the law, the reimbursement income might be appropriated directly to the board of regents for debt service on behalf of the institutions of higher education. The great advantage of this new arrangement was the general assembly might now authorize capital improvements for higher education to be paid for by revenue bonds, without the periodic submission of bond issues to the voters.

This constitutional amendment of 1968 was one of the major contributions of Governor Rhodes to higher education in Ohio. Under this new arrangement and upon his recommendation, a further capital improvement program of $186 million was authorized in the biennium 1969–71. In 1971–73, another $164 million in capital improvements was authorized by the Republican-dominated legislature, although there was now a Democratic governor.

The Rhodes influence was still evident in 1971 even though he ceased to be governor in January of that year—Ohio authorized capital improvements amounting to $770 million for higher education. With matching grants under the federal government's Higher Education Facilities Act of 1963, the total capital improvement invested in those years came to about one billion dollars.

**Operating support**

When Rhodes became governor in January of 1963, the total state appropriations from tax funds in support of higher education came to about $55 million. In the first biennium of the Rhodes' administration, the general assembly appropriated $60.5 million for the fiscal year 1964 and $67.7 million for the 1970–71 school year.

In 1967, the governor—in private conference with legislative leaders and in the preparation of legislative language for committee action—adopted a new approach to legislative action. He advocated that the appropriation measure should be combined with the tax recommendation into a single bill. In addition, substantive language affecting the expenditure of higher education funds and school foundation funds was included in the appropriation/tax measure. Parts of the bill might be considered by different committees in each house of the legislature. Governor Rhodes, however, insisted that each house should vote on the measure as a whole. This strategy was devised in order to make clear that appropriation and tax provisions of the law were interrelated and constituted a total package designed to avoid any discrepancy between revenues and expenditures. This practice was to be followed in subsequent years by Governor Gilligan, by Governor Rhodes (1975–83), and by Governor Celeste.

*I*n the 1969–71 legislative years, Rhodes endorsed another new feature for higher education financing in Ohio, the creation of the Ohio Instructional Grant Program. This new student aid program was designed to ensure that no undergraduate student from a family below the median Ohio income would have to pay any increase in student instructional fees. Instructional grants were also made available to undergraduate students who were Ohio students enrolled in Ohio's private colleges. Ohio began a student financial assistance program before the federal government's Educational Amendments of 1972, which inaugurated grants to states aiding students' financial assistance programs.

In 1968 and 1969, under recommendation of Governor Rhodes, Ohio began two other programs to assist private colleges and universities in Ohio. In 1968, the general assembly enacted legislation making it possible for private colleges and universities to borrow funds for capital improvements through state agency whose bonds were exempt from federal government income taxes. This

The Governor, circa 1980.

arrangement substantially reduced the debt service for private institutions. In 1969, the state began to subsidize the costs of the medical school at Case Western Reserve University in recognition of the service rendered by the school and its affiliated hospitals in meeting the health care needs of the state's largest city.

A final change in law conferred the status of a body politic and corporate upon each state university in Ohio. Ohio University and Miami University, under original state charters, had both been designated a body. Now in the 1960s, some 150 years later, all the state universities were established as government corporations, different in many ways from a regular state government agency.

Only those familiar with the burden of state centralized administrative controls over higher education—controls criticized strongly by a group headed by Milton S. Eisenhower in 1959—would understand the far-reaching nature of the "management revolution" that benefited all the state universities and wrought by Governor Rhodes in his first two years in office.

## Summary

The public system grew from six universities in 1962 to twelve universities, two independent medical colleges, and twenty-two permanent university branches—thirty-six higher education centers offering bachelors and higher degrees.

Operating appropriations increased from $55,620,000 in fiscal 1963 to $672, 257,000 in fiscal 1979.

Total appropriations per full-time-equivalent student increased from $645 in 1963 to $1812 in 1979.

In 1980–81 Ohio ranked forty-fourth in per-capital appropriations for higher education and thirty-fourth for percent change over the period.

The state subsidy in the 1981–82 biennium was calculated on the basis of a sixty-seven percent/thirty-three percent sharing of costs by the state and the student.

Total operating expenditures climbed from approximately $150 million in 1963 to $1.4 billion in fiscal 1970. (This includes expenditures on community colleges and technical institutes reviewed in the next section.)

The physical plant of the sixty-one institutions with sixty-five permanent campuses contained more than 1,400 buildings totaling 64,225,000 gross square feet at an estimated value of $3 billion. These figures include community colleges and technical institutes.

The Ohio Instructional Grant Program initiated during Governor Rhodes' second term in office and implemented in fiscal 1972, grew from a total of $14,586,417 aiding 29,970 students to $26,728,646 and 56,349 students in fiscal 1980. These grants were distributed to students enrolled in both public and private colleges, universities, diploma schools of nursing, and proprietary schools.

## PUBLIC HIGHER EDUCATION APPROPRIATIONS AND ENROLLMENTS FOR UNIVERSITIES

| Year | Appropriations | Enrollments |
|------|---------------|-------------|
| 1962–63 | $47,379,000 | 102,066 |
| 1963–64 | 51,691,000 | 110,190 |
| 1964–65 | 58,413,000 | 122,213 |
| 1965–66 | 71,240,000 | 144,267 |
| 1966–67 | 77,895,000 | 154,286 |
| 1967–68 | 124,245,000 | 180,512 |
| 1968–69 | 150,182,000 | 193,078 |
| 1969–70 | 179,895,000 | 210,440 |
| 1970–71 | 190,151,000 | 218,818 |
| 1971–72 | 211,089,000 | 222,406 |
| 1972–73 | 223,965,000 | 220,657 |
| 1973–74 | 247,522,000 | 220,351 |
| 1974–75 | 279,097,000 | 224,552 |
| 1975–76 | 317,402,000 | 234,709 |
| 1976–77 | 344,780,000 | 233,659 |
| 1977–78 | 377,424,000 | 236,459 |
| 1978–79 | 418,531,000 | 232,656 |
| 1979–80 | | 239,264 |
| 1980–81 | | 250,844 |

(The figures listed include the four-year term of
Governor Gilligan)

All but four years of the above period were during the
Rhodes administrations.

## ENROLLMENTS BY PUBLIC UNIVERSITY
*1965–1984*

| State Universities | 1984 | 1965 |
|---|---|---|
| Akron | 26,270 | 10,278 |
| Bowling Green | 17,762 | 9,901 |
| Central State | 2,321 | 2,194 |
| Cincinnati | 29,757 | 24,512 |
| Cleveland | 17,334 | 6,026 |
| Kent | 19,299 | 14,833 |
| Miami | 15,040 | 9,937 |
| Ohio State | 52,028 | 37,089 |
| Ohio University | 14,462 | 14,517 |
| Shawnee | | |
| Toledo | 20,616 | 10,464 |
| Wright | 14,100 | 4,516 |
| Youngstown | 15,204 | |
| Medical College of Toledo | 733 | |
| **Total** | **244,326** | **144,267** |
| | | |
| Branches | 30,045 | 18,238 |

The leadership and vision of Governor Rhodes
in relationship to the needs of industry and business
for professional people and the needs of the people
of Ohio to participate in quality higher education is
remarkably clear. Under his administrations more

money was invested in higher education than was expended during the previous 160 years of the state's history.

# New learning

When James Rhodes became governor of Ohio, technical education was in its infancy. In 1959, with strong support from business and industry, the Division of Vocational Education in the State Department of Education encouraged the legislature to pass legislation initiating two-year post high school technical education programs under the auspices of the State Department of Education. The legislation passed both the house and the senate. It was vetoed, however, by Governor DiSalle at the request of three college presidents.

When the Russian sputnik ascended into the heavens, our nation panicked about the technological lag in relationship to Russia. Funds to upgrade the technology in the U.S. were made available in many areas. An allocation of federal funds was made to the Division of Vocational Education in the State Department of Education, to establish training for highly skilled occupations.

From left, Roger Cloud, auditor; Ted Brown, secretary of state; Rhodes; John Brown, lieutenant governor; and John Herbert, treasurer.

The Division of Vocational Education, under the leadership of Dr. Byrl R. Shoemaker, made a study of technical education programs over the nation and made use of the new monies to initiate two-year post high school technical education programs. The initial two programs were established in 1960 within the facilities of Springfield High School in Springfield, Ohio, under the leadership of Richard Brinkman, and in a surplus elementary education building in the public school district of Lorain, Ohio, under the leadership of Dr. Max Learner. Brinkman was then the superintendent of the new Springfield Clark County Joint Vocational School District. Dr. Lerner was then the director of vocational education in the Lorain Public Schools.

This was only the beginning of a program that grew into technical and community colleges that in 1984 enrolled 107,218 students. Governor Rhodes endorsed and encouraged the development of two-year post high school technical education centers on the basis that it related to his program of "Jobs and Progress."

The massive expansion of technology in industry and business forced people in the professions to a higher level of performance. In many cases, professional people no longer had the time to do many of the lesser skilled areas of work, which they had previously performed. As an example, those who were graduating from engineering classes formerly had to spend two to three years on a drafting board before they could truly function in an engineering capacity.

With the increase in technology, the engineering colleges could not spend the amount of time on the basic drafting and design skills as provided in earlier years. Thus, in many professions the increased levels of technology opened up a whole new area of employment. Jobs in this new level of employment required more technical knowledge and skills in the areas of design, development, and testing than were required for the skilled trades and less than required for the professions.

In comparison with the highly skilled crafts of manufacturing, construction, repair, and servicing, the technicians were to assume all areas of support for the professional people. The technician level programs in Ohio were designed on the concept that wherever there was a profession and wherever the profession would accept and assist in the design of the program for paraprofessionals, such a program could be established. Acceptance of such technicians by the professionals and participation of the professionals in the design of the technician training programs were essential.

With support from Governor Rhodes, the Division of Vocational Education in the State Department of Education worked with industry and business to design new technical education programs. Thirteen post high school technical educational centers were in operation by 1967, when the state board of regents was established. Most of them were established in cooperation with, but educationally and administratively separate from, the area joint vocational school districts, which will be discussed in a later chapter.

Dr. Harold Boles, Dean of the College of Engineering at The Ohio State University, assisted the Division of Vocational Education in the State Department of Education to design engineering technician training programs. He indicated that professional engineers graduating from his program at the university needed technicians in order to make their work economical and effective.

Dr. Shoemaker in the Division of Vocational Education, State Department of Education, was assigned by the state superintendent to work with the federally funded Appalachian Regional Commission, which provided funds to improve life in the Appalachian area that covered parts of several states. Dr. Shoemaker was successful in getting this commission to provide funding to add buildings to area vocational education centers planned, and committed specifically for the two-year post high school technical education.

In 1967, there were thirteen two-year post high

school technical educational centers operating under the Division of Vocational Education. Also, there were two community colleges and one technical institute developed under the legislation passed in 1960 authorizing such community colleges. One community college was located in Lorain County, developed under the leadership of Dr. Max Lerner, one in Cleveland, and the technical institute center in Jefferson County.

The thirteen technical education centers operating under the Division of Vocational Education, however, had a problem. The centers had only a limited amount of funds provided under the Vocational Education Acts of Congress to assist them with construction, equipment, and operation. Also, the Division did not have the authority to grant "Associate Degrees" for two-year post high school programs. Even though industry supported the thirteen technical education centers and their graduates were quickly assimilated into industry and business, there were no funds available for growth of this new level of education.

As the board of regents was developed and became the leadership force for higher education, Dr. John Millet Chancellor of the board of regents determined the two-year post high school centers should become a part of the program of the board of regents. He stated this board could provide the associate degree for those completing the two-year programs and could provide significant funding for the expansion of building, equipment, and operation. Thus, even though the leadership at several universities had opposed the development of the two-year post high school centers, the board of regents saw the need for graduates from such centers, and the opportunities they provided youth in keeping with the governor's goal of "a higher education facility within thirty-five miles of every citizen in the state."

The control of the thirteen technical education centers, developed by the Division of Vocational Education in the State Department of Education, was turned over to the board of regents. A "Memorandum of Agreement" was developed between the board of regents and the state board of education that continued the assistance of the Division of Vocational Education with the technical education centers.

The additional funds and the availability of the associate degree from the board of regents brought about a rapid expansion of technical education for Ohio. The chancellor of the board of regents encouraged such centers to expand their goals and to become community colleges, offering both two-year post high technical education and transfer credit for the first two years of college.

Statistics show that in 1984, twenty-three technical and community colleges enrolled 107,218 students. The twenty-three technical institutes and community colleges, plus the fourteen state universities with their branches, enabled Rhodes to achieve his goal of a center of higher education within thirty-five miles of every resident of Ohio.

Information on the growth of technical institutes and community colleges is as follows:

# ℐechnical institutes and community colleges:

| Year | Appropriations | Enrollments |
|------|---------------|-------------|
| 1962–63 | $8,241,000 | 13,091 |
| 1963–64 | 8,759,000 | 18,292 |
| 1964–65 | 9,255,000 | 26,194 |
| 1965–66 | 13,624,000 | 29,665 |
| 1966–67 | 15,205,000 | 33,273 |
| 1967–68 | 24,352,000 | 41,308 |
| 1968–69 | 26,545,000 | 47,429 |
| 1969–70 | 60,833,000 | 55,092 |
| 1970–71 | 52,365,000 | 60,542 |
| 1971–72 | 81,826,000 | 68,131 |
| 1972–73 | 96,462,000 | 72,281 |
| 1973–74 | 116,595,000 | 77,747 |
| 1974–75 | 140,635,000 | 84,876 |
| 1975–76 | 158,455,000 | 104,983 |
| 1976–77 | 191,093,000 | 112,208 |
| 1977–78 | 216,652,000 | 116,810 |
| 1978–79 | 253,726,000 | 118,531 |

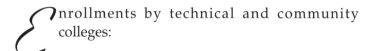
*E*nrollments by technical and community colleges:

| Colleges | 1984 |
|---|---|
| Belmont Technical | 1,901 |
| Central Ohio Technical | 1,446 |
| Cincinnati Technical | 4,500 |
| Clark State Community | 2,200 |
| Columbus State Community | 9,520 |
| Cuyahoga Community | 22,378 |
| Edison State Community | 2,652 |
| Hocking Technical | 4,107 |
| Jefferson Technical | 1,410 |
| Lakeland Community | 1,840 |
| Lima Technical | 1,945 |
| Lorain County Community | 6,089 |
| Marion Technical | 1,351 |
| Muskingum Area Technical | 1,944 |
| North Central Technical | 1,835 |
| Northwest Technical | 1,869 |
| Owens Technical | 6,653 |
| Rio Grande Community | 1,884 |
| Sinclair Community | 16,615 |
| Southern State Community | 1,288 |
| Stark Technical | 3,275 |
| Terra Technical | 2,614 |
| Washington Technical | 1,902 |
| **Total** | **107,218** |

Governor Rhodes understood quickly the importance of this new level of education and its relationship to the "Jobs and Progress" goal of his administration. He gave it full support while the administrators of colleges and universities tended to see technical education as competition for funds. This new area of education was initiated and developed by the Division of Vocational Education in the State Department of Education. Its growth to the level of effective service to industry, business, and the people of Ohio, and to credit courses for transfer to colleges and universities, came under the Rhodes' administrations, and a totally new level of education was introduced into the state.

# Vocational education

James Rhodes' interests in education were not limited to higher education. He was interested in the needs of all people and the needs of industry and business for all levels of workers. His goal of "Jobs and Progress" called for an educated work force and for the development of the skilled workers that are the backbone of our progress to prosperity.

Rhodes was particularly aware of the statistic that forty-seven percent of high school graduates started college. He was also aware that only eighteen percent of the jobs available in the workforce required a college degree and questioned what happened to the fifty-three percent that did not go to college, the dropouts from high school, and the dropouts from the college program. He firmly believed that, "a high school graduate has the right to expect a diploma in one hand and a job in the other on graduation day."

In his book, *Alternative to a Decadent Society* (Charles Merrill Publishers, 1969) the governor said, "Our

The Governor at highway
dedication, mid-1960s.

education system is a hundred years out of date. We have
answered the challenge of education by making it more
difficult—not more relevant. We hear a lot of talk about
the importance of the individual, but the system is locked
in to the teaching of subjects, and the system has bowed
to the snobbery of the limited group able to achieve in a
few of the favored disciplines."

At another point in the same book he stated, "The
nation is locked in a fierce struggle with itself, and is
hanging on the ropes from the deadly blows of creatures
and conditions of our own making. Slowly but surely
we have created the problems that we must now solve
and the time is running out. We have hitched our wagon
to a star, but our feet are not touching the ground. The
warm moist breeding conditions of a decadent society are

present in abundance. Left alone, these conditions will multiply and will threaten our very existence."

His interest in vocational education was motivated not only by the needs of industry and business for trained workers but by such studies as the one made with 57,116 sophomores and juniors in 206 high schools. The study reported that 72.6 percent desired to have vocational and technical education programs. One of his well-known statements was, "The general education program leads only to general unemployment." His creative and forceful views on "education for work" are well documented in the above listed book.

The growth and development of vocational education in Ohio during the Rhodes years has been called the greatest success story in the history of education in Ohio. The phenomenal growth of vocational education can be attributed to: the interest and support given the programs by Governor Rhodes; the bipartisan support in the legislature; and the efforts of the Division of Vocational Education in the State Department of Education, under the leadership of Dr. Byrl R. Shoemaker.

*I*n 1962, vocational programs providing adequate training programs for skilled trades, business and office, and marketing were limited to the six major cities. This was due to the fact that most of the other 720 districts in Ohio did not have enough student base or tax base to support a broad program that met the varying needs of the students or industry and business. On the other hand, the programs for agriculture and home economics were limited to the small cities and rural areas. Yet the cities had opportunities for landscape gardening and nursery work and agriculture-based industries. The girls in the major cities often had more needs for instruction in family life, nutrition and childcare, and money management than their counterparts in the rural areas.

The state legislature passed a measure in 1963, signed into law by Governor Rhodes, that permitted school districts to join together and provide broad programs of vocational education, in joint vocational school districts. When James Rhodes became governor, the Division of Vocational Education, State Department of Education, was promoting this new educational opportunity with funds available only from limited federal vocational education funding.

Rhodes, after signing the authorizing state legislation for expansion into law, immediately saw its application to the needs of industry and business for better-trained people and the needs of people for job skills.

At the time Rhodes was inaugurated into office, the vocational program in Ohio was as follows:

- Served only 47,240 youth in our public school vocational programs.

- Served only 92,582 adults in upgrading programs to assist them to hold or advance in their jobs, using the same facilities in the late afternoon and evening that were used by youth in the daytime.

- Served only 347 youth in programs planned for disadvantaged students.

- Had vocational centers with any breadth of programming available in only six major cities.

- Had no area vocational education centers or joint vocational districts.

- Had never invested state funds in the construction and equipping of vocational education facilities.

- Provided only 1,134 units of vocational education under the state foundation program.

- Post high school technical education programs enrolled only 692 full-time students.

*D*ue to the support of Governor Rhodes, the bi-partisan efforts of the legislature, and the work of the Division of Vocational Education in the State Department of Education, the state superintendent and the state board of education, vocational education programs showed a phenomenal growth over the four Rhodes' administrations. The efforts had the support of the governor, the legislature, the public, and industry and business, but often faced opposition from local educational administrators who did not want to cooperate with other districts in a joint vocational school district or in a compact type of organization. Growth and development was not limited to the suburban and rural areas but saw major additions of vocational education in the major cities.

Dr. Byrl R. Shoemaker, Director of Vocational and Career Education, often accompanied the governor on his visits to industries or businesses that were considering locating or expanding in Ohio. The services of vocational education were a drawing card for such industries. As an example, General Motors Corp. indicated it would consider installing an engine building plant in a facility it had abandoned in Dayton, Ohio, if the state would provide some roads and training for the new work force.

Governor Rhodes sent the director of vocational education to meet with them and to give them whatever help they needed in training the new work force. With the cooperation of the vocational program centers in the Dayton Public Schools, the training was accomplished for the more than 1,000 new employees.

When the president of General Motors Corp. dedicated the plant, he indicated it was the smoothest opening they ever had, due to the training provided for the workers.

The vocational education programs in 1979, in Rhodes' fourth term, showed an astounding growth and development over the programs existing in 1963. Some of the significant achievements as of 1979 were as follows:

- 282,528 high school youth were enrolled in public school vocational education programs.

- 212,937 adults were enrolled in part-time vocational programs in the public schools.

- 42,496 post-high youth were enrolled in full-time vocational or technical programs.

- 28,760 disadvantaged youth were served by job training vocational programs planned specifically for this type of student.

- 9,659 14- and 15-year-old dropout prone youth were enrolled in an occupational work adjustment program in which they gained work experience for pay.

- 50,577 youth and adults worked in business and industry as a part of their vocational program and earned over $69 million, "earning as they learned."

- 287,490 youth in grades K-10 were provided education for career choice through the career education program in the public schools.

- 97.4% of all youth in the state had an adequate vocational program available. (The goal of 100% was achieved in 1983).

- 57.1% of all youth in the last two years of high school were enrolled in vocational programs with the majority, 40.1%, enrolled in job training and the remainder in vocational home economics programs.

- In the eight major cities, 77% of all youth in the last two years of high school were enrolled in approved vocational programs, with the majority, 57%, enrolled in job training programs.

- A total of fifty joint vocational school districts had been organized to provide broad vocational programs through cooperation between school districts. Forty-nine had voted the funds required for construction and operation and the forty-nine were in operation.

- The 720 school districts had been organized into 102 vocational planning districts on the basis of the standards recommended by the Division of Vocational Education and approved by the State Board of Vocational Education.

- The 102 vocational districts had been organized in twenty-four consortiums to assist new or expanding industries and businesses to identify training needs and to use the vocational training facilities in the consortium areas effectively.

- The Division of Vocational Education was cooperating with the Department of Economic and Community Development in providing information and services to industries considering Ohio as a location.

- $528,438,416 in state, federal, and local funds had been expended since 1965 for the construction and equipment of vocational education facilities.

*E*arly in his first term, Governor Rhodes identified the growth of jobs through the expansion of industry and business as the only successful solution to growing welfare rolls. In attracting new industry and business to Ohio, he learned that the availability of trained people and of facilities to train persons without the skills for the new jobs, was an important factor in the decision of industry or business locating in the state. In addition, a review of the unemployed revealed that few of them had gained work skills necessary to make them employable in a modern technological world in which less than five percent of the jobs were in the unskilled range.

While Governor Rhodes greatly expanded higher education, it was recognized that the large majority of the jobs did not require a baccalaureate degree. He determined, therefore, the expansion of vocational education was important to both the youth entering the work force and out-of-school youth and adults in the work force without skills needed by employers.

Governor Rhodes spoke out boldly in support of local levies to provide the matching funds to build, equip, and operate the expanded vocational programs. He encouraged business, industry, and the public to provide youth and adults with an opportunity to prepare for workfare instead of welfare. Throughout Ohio, he promoted the concept of youth graduating from high school with a diploma in one hand and a job in the other.

The assistance from the state or federal funds for building and equipment was not given indiscriminately. Districts first had to meet the standard of size or join with other districts in a jointure or compact arrangement, then vote the money needed locally to match state or federal money made available for building and equipment. Both parties in the legislature supported the effort to bring about this major change in the educational services.

Initially, there was no requirement forcing the 720 districts to make a plan involving all of the districts in a pattern that would bring vocational services to all youth. In 1969, Rhodes proposed landmark legislation that required the establishment of an adequate program of vocational education for all youth within the state, with the facilities to serve adults as well.

The proposed legislation was passed with bipartisan support in the legislature in 1969. The new legislation required the state board of education to establish standards for an adequate program of vocation and to prepare a plan for vocational education for Ohio in which no district was left out.

From the State Bond Issue No.1, passed in 1968, Governor Rhodes recommended the allocation of $75 million to match locally voted funds for the construction and equipment of vocational education facilities. In subsequent years, additional funds were provided by the state legislature to assist with the completion of the vocational education facilities.

Governor Rhodes' concepts concerning the importance of vocational education for both the individual and the economy were well defined in his book *Alternative to a Decadent Society,* referred to earlier in this chapter and further defined in his book, *Vocational Education and Guidance a System for the Seventies.*

The names of the forty-nine joint vocational districts established under the Rhodes' administration are:

Apollo JVSD, Cridersville, Allen County.
Ashland County-West Holmes JVSD, Ashland,
    Ashland County.
Ashtabula County JVSD, Ashtabula,
    Ashtabula County.
Belmont-Harrison Area JVSD, St. Clairesville,
    Belmont County.
Buckeye JVSD, New Philadelphia,
    Tuscarawas County.

Butler County JVSD, Hamilton-Middletown,
    Butler County.
Central Ohio JVSD, Plain City, Madison County.
Columbia County JVSD, Lisbon, Columbia County.
Coshocton County JVSD, Coshocton,
    Coshocton County.
Cuyahoga Valley JVSD, Brecksville,
    Cuyahoga County.
Delaware County JVSD, Delaware,
    Delaware County.
Eastland JVSD, Groveport, Franklin County.
EHOVE JVSD, Milan, Erie County.
Four County JVSD, Archbold, Henry County.
Gallia-Jackson-Vinton JVSD, Rio Grande,
    Gallia County.
Great Oaks JVSD, Cincinnati, Hamilton County.
    (four centers)
Greene County JVSD, Xenia, Greene County.
Jefferson County JVSD, Bloomington,
    Jefferson County.
Knox County JVSD, Mount Vernon, Knox County.
Lake County JVSD, Painesville, Lake County.
Lawrence County JVSD, Chesapeake,
    Lawrence County.
Licking Co, JVSD, Newark, Licking County.
Lorain County JVSD, Oberlin, Lorian County.
Mahoning County JVSD, Canfield,
    Mahoning County.
Maplewood Area JVSD, Ravenna, Portage County.
Medina County JVSD, Medina, Medina County.
Mid-East Ohio JVSD, Zanesville,
    Muskingum County.

Montgomery County JVSD, Clayton,
    Montgomery County.
Ohio Hi-Point JVSD, Bellefontaine, Logan County.
Penta County JVSD, Perrysberg, Wood County.
Pickaway-Ross County JVSD, Chillicothe,
    Ross County.
Pike County Area JVSD, Piketon, Pike County.
Pioneer JVSD, Shelby, Richland County.
Polaris JVSD, Middleburg, Cuyhoga County.
Portage Lakes JVSD, Greensburg, Summit County.
Scioto County JVSD, Lucasville, Scioto County.
Southern Hills JVSD, Georgetown, Brown County.
Springfield-Clark County JVSD, Springfield,
    Clark County.
Stark County Area JVSD, Massillon, Stark County.
Tri County JVSD, Nelsonville, Athens County.
Tri-Rivers JVSD, Marion, Marion County.
Trumbull County JVSD, Warren, Trumbull County.
US Grant JVSD, Bethel, Clermont County.
Upper Valley JVSD, Piqua, Miami County.
Vanguard-Sentinel JVSD, Fremont,
    Sandusky County.
Vantage JVSD, Van Wert, Van Wert County.
Warren County JVSD, Lebanon, Warren County.
Washington County JVSD, Marietta,
    Washington County.
Wayne County JVSD, Smithville, Wayne County.

*A*s the vocational education programs were expanding, it became obvious that youth needed a better pattern of career choice than was available to the youth in the public schools. In 1969,

Rhodes supported concepts promoted by the Division of Vocational Education, State Department of Education, for the initiation of a career guidance program. His concepts for a career guidance program were outlined in his book, *Vocational Education and Guidance—A System for the Seventies* (Charles E Merrill Publishers, 1970). Governor Rhodes took copies of this book to China and gave them to the Chinese leaders with whom he met.

This career guidance movement in Ohio predated the massive national interest and focused upon this topic in the 1970s and gained Ohio national recognition. Experience over the years suggests the bold action initiated by Rhodes and supported by both political parties in the legislature resulted in significant change and improvements in public education programs

The expansions of higher education and technical education required voting by the people for funds on a statewide basis. The expansion of vocational education, however, required much more direct support by the voters of the various localities where the new vocational facilities were to be built. Every facility had to be voted upon by the electorate and required an increase in local taxes. They had to vote the matching money and their share of operating funds before any state or federal funds would be provided. The electorate, therefore, had to indicate its support for the expansion of these new opportunities for youth and adults.

The state board of education was charged by legislation, and promoted by Governor Rhodes, with the responsibility of setting standards for the minimum scope of program to be provided by the new centers. It was also responsible for setting standards and for the implementation of a plan that would see that all school districts in the state were organized into vocational planning districts that met the minimum numbers of students established by the legislation.

The 702 school districts in the state had to cooperate with each other to meet the state standards that established a minimum scope of curriculum but left the identification of the specific programs to the new vocational district. The school districts were encouraged to use the assistance of industry and business in determining the programs to be offered. A number of educational leaders at the state and local district levels, such as the county superintendents and the superintendents of a number of small cities, supported the movement to provide for the growth of vocational education. The majority of the superintendents in smaller districts opposed the effort but followed the regulations of the state board of education.

The moving forces were a bold and resourceful governor; the Division of Vocational Education in the State Department of Education, which provided the educational concepts and procedures; the establishment of high standards by the state board of education; and the bipartisan effort in the state legislature. Both the Democratic and Republican members of the legislature supported the legislation for change and provided the required state funds over a long period of years to complete the goal of "providing an adequate program of vocational education for all youth and adults in Ohio."

The goal of an adequate vocational program was achieved in 1983, the year after Governor Rhodes left office for the last time. The remarkable achievement gained national recognition as the first state to achieve such a goal.

The effort stretched over many years, twenty years from the passage of the legislation permitting the establishment of joint vocational school districts. It was proved that major educational changes would be made if there were educational leadership with concepts that would be recognized by the electorate as sound, and bold state leadership in the governor's office and the legislature.

The vocational programs in Ohio are a tribute to a great governor and legislature, which gave support. It could and must happen again for other areas of education.

# Profit is no dirty word

Governor Rhodes' primary goal throughout his administration was to get as many Ohioans as possible to become jobholders and taxpayers instead of tax consumers. He consistently pursued policies and programs that encouraged the growth of industry, business, and commerce to provide more and better private sector jobs for all Ohioans.

The slogan, "Profit is Not a Dirty Word in Ohio," set the theme of his administrations and established a positive attitude toward industrial growth.

In his first eight years, through his department of development, Ohio assisted 212 companies locate or expand in Ohio, providing nearly 50,000 new jobs. Despite a faltering economy, the governor and the development department scored gains of expansions and relocations in the second eight years that continued to benefit Ohioans.

Governor Rhodes cutting ribbon at state fair during the 1960s. That's finance director Richard Krabach at far left.

## Hunting jobs: highlights of the second eight years

| Company | Location | Jobs | Year |
| --- | --- | --- | --- |
| Adria Laboraties | Columbus, Franklin | 50 | 1981 |
| AIResearch Mfg. Co. | Sandusky, Erie | 50 | 1979 |
| AMC/Jeep Corp. | Toledo, Lucas | 2,000 | 1978 |
| America Honda Co. | Dayton, Montgomery | 20 | 1976 |
| Anthony Candy Co. | Columbus, Franklin | 42 | 1982 |
| Ariel Corporation | Mt. Vernon, Knox | 75 | 1980 |

| Company | Location | Jobs | Year |
|---|---|---|---|
| Ashland-Publicker | South Point, Lawrence | 150 | 1980 |
| Bellemar Parts Industries | Marysville, Union | 200 | 1981 |
| Buckeye Printing Ink Co. | Columbus, Franklin | 18 | 1982 |
| Control Data Corp. | Toledo, Lucas | 300 | 1981 |
| Cessna Aircraft/ McCauley Aviation Division | Vandalia, Montgomery | 328 | 1979 |
| Chrysler Corp. XM-1 Tank | Lima, Allen | 1,500 | 1980 |
| Church and Dwight Co. | Old Fort, Seneca | 65 | 1978 |
| Cincinnati City | Cincinnati, Hamilton | 916 | 1982 |
| Combustion Engineering | Cleveland, Cuyahoga | 300 | 1976 |
| R.R. Donnely Corp. | Willard, Huron | 1,180 | 1980 |
| Emery Airfreight Co. | Vandalia, Montgomery | 500 | 1981 |
| Ford Motor Co. | Batavia, Clermont | 3,400 | 1977 |
| Fujitec Co. | Lebanon, Warren | 500 | 1981 |
| General Motors (2 Exp.) | Moraine, Montgomery | 6,000 | 1981 |
| Gilford. Instruments | Lorain, Lorain | 60 | 1978 |

| Company | Location | Jobs | Year |
|---|---|---|---|
| Globe Union Inc. | Oregon, Lucas | 140 | 1981 |
| Godfrey & Wing | Cleveland, Cuyahoga | 38 | 1981 |
| Goodyear Aerospace Corp. / Goodyear Tire & Rubber | Akron, Summit | 500 | 1981 |
| Gould Inc. | Napoleon, Henry | 50 | 1978 |
| Griffin Wheel Co. | Groveport, Franklin | 200 | 1979 |
| Gruman Flexible | Delaware, Delaware | 300 | 1981 |
| G. & W. Industries | Cleveland, Cuyahoga | 88 | 1982 |
| Helios | Newark, Licking | 200 | 1978 |
| Honda of America Inc. | Marysville, Union | 2,000 | 1980 |
| Honsel-Werke AG/ Hayes Albion Foundry | Tiffin, Seneca | 130 | 1978 |
| Hunt Energy, Inc | Salem, Columbiana | 526 | 1982 |
| Hunger Co. | Rossford, Wood | 350 | 1981 |
| INCA Presswood | Dover, Tuscarawas | 40 | 1978 |
| Jackson Co. Improvement Corp. | Jackson, Jackson | 175 | 1982 |

| Company | Location | Jobs | Year |
|---|---|---|---|
| Jeno's Inc. | Wellston, Jackson | 1,000 | 1981 |
| Johnson Controls | Holland, Lucas | 300 | 1979 |
| Keithley Instruments | Solon, Cuyahoga | 175 | 1979 |
| K-Mart | Warren, Trumbull | 500 | 1978 |
| K.S.H. Inc. | Xenia, Greene | 84 | 1982 |
| Mac Tools Inc. | Georgetown & Columbus | 350 | 1978 |
| Marietta, Metals | Marietta, Washington | 88 | 1981 |
| C.H. Masland & Sons | Sidney, Shelby | 160 | 1981 |
| Medex Inc. | Hilliard, Franklin | 200 | 1980 |
| Merrilat Industries (New & Expansion) | Jackson, Jackson | 200 | 1980 |
| Miami Valley Publishing Co. | Fairborn, Montgomery | 82 | 1982 |
| Montgomery-Ward Co. | Sharonville, Hamilton | 750 | 1977 |
| Molan Duplex | Bowerston, Harrison | 78 | 1981 |
| Norwalk Furniture Corp. | Norwalk, Huron | 200 | 1981 |
| Ohio Pure Foods | Akron, Summit | 100 | 1979 |

| Company | Location | Jobs | Year |
|---------|----------|------|------|
| Ohio Steel Tube Co. | Shelby, Richland | 110 | 1979 |
| Parker Hannifin Corp. | Lewisburg, Preble | 50 | 1979 |
| Perfection Mfg. Co. | Mansfield, Richland | 150 | 1979 |
| Permco, Inc. | Streetsboro, Portage | 80 | 1982 |
| Perstorp | Toledo, Lucas | 30 | 1977 |
| Platt Mfg. Co. | Dayton, Montgomery | 37 | 1982 |
| Pre-Finished Metals | Toledo, Lucas | 50 | 1980 |
| Presrite | Cleveland, Cuyahoga | 45 | 1982 |
| Process Equip. Co. | Tipp City, Miami | 50 | 1980 |
| Pultrustions Corp. | Aurora, Portage | 90 | 1981 |
| Ray-O-Vac Corp | Lancaster, Fairfield | 350 | 1981 |
| Republic Steel Corp. | Canton, Stark | 70 | 1978 |
| RMI Co. | Ashtabula, Ashtabula | 75 | 1979 |
| Schuler-Leukart, Inc | Columbus, Franklin | 100 | 1980 |
| Stanley Electric Co. Ltd. | London, Madison | 200 | 1980 |

| Company | Location | Jobs | Year |
|---|---|---|---|
| Stroh Brewery Co. | Fremont, Sandusky | 300 | 1979 |
| Sheller-Glober Corp. | Cleveland, Cuyahoga | 138 | 1980 |
| Shopsmith | Vandalia, Montgomery | 1,000 | 1981 |
| Tamarkin Co. | Youngstown, Mahoning | 300 | 1981 |
| Technicare | Solon, Cuyahoga | 500 | 1981 |
| Teledyne | Toledo, Lucas | 318 | 1981 |
| 3-Sigma, Inc. | Covington, Miami | 35 | 1980 |
| Tempered Glass Specialists Inc. | Antwerp, Paulding | 60 | 1981 |
| Timken | Canton, Stark | 1,000 | 1981 |
| Tremco Inc. | Columbus, Franklin | 140 | 1981 |
| TRW Corp. | Lindhurst, Cuyahoga | 300 | 1981 |
| Union Metal Mfg. Co. | Canton, Stark | 100 | 1982 |
| United Color Press of Dayton Inc. | Monroe, Butler | 401 | 1981 |
| Ward/Kraft Forms | Fredricktown, Knox | 60 | 1980 |
| Wheeling Trueing Tool | Chardon, Geauga | 30 | 1979 |

| Company | Location | Jobs | Year |
|---------|----------|------|------|
| Yellow Springs Instr. | Yellow Springs, Greene | 165 | 1979 |

**Total companies—82; jobs—33, 492**

In addition to job hunting (managed in Rhodes' development department's economic development division that included travel and tourism, small business assistance, and a film bureau), the department was organized into: A community development division (housing, planning, local services, weatherization, and Appalachia); a minority business development division; and an international trade division (with offices in Brussels and Tokyo). Jim Rhodes made job development in Ohio into a multimillion-dollar effort, and it still is.

### Growth and Improvements in Recreation and Conservation

Around the conference room outside the office, during his first term as governor, there were displayed architectual illustrations of lodges and individual cabins identified for rural areas of the state. These were ideas that Rhodes had conceived as future recreation centers for the state. Members of his staff told him that such planning was a waste of time and effort. They said, "The people of Ohio would never make use of such elaborate recreation areas. They are nothing but a dream." The governor listened but did not believe. All of the lodges and recreation centers conceived by Rhodes for the people of Ohio were built and are used extensively today by

Ohioans and visitors from other states. They told him it couldn't be done, but he did it.

Even members of his staff deemed many of the accomplishments of the Rhodes' administrations impossible. He hired leadership that believed they could be done, however, and together they did it. The parks and recreation areas developed during the Rhodes' years have added much to the opportunities for the people to appreciate the beauty of our own state.

The scope of Governor Rhodes' interests and motivations are somewhat unbelievable. For a man committed to "Jobs and Progress," he also had a concern for the things in life that brought joy and happiness and a higher quality of life. He was a leader with ideas and the energy and ability to put them into practice.

*B*efore 1962, the state parks in Ohio were operated only seasonally, with many areas padlocked and unusable. Under Rhodes, policies and ideas were instituted which provided facilities and activities for outdoor recreation throughout the year. They were varied facilities and activities to meet all interests—facilities and activities that provided for family fun and that made them proud of their state. Over and over again, he proved that he was concerned about the people of the state, as only an honest and dedicated person could.

In 1963, at the beginning of his first administration, the new governor promised a bold $100 million program to satisfy the ever-increasing demands for outdoor recreation. This promise was attained and surpassed. Some $175,000,000 of improvements for outdoor opportunities and natural resources were completed, under construction, or ready to be put under construction at the end of the first eight years.

During that time, 50,000 additional acres of public recreation land and 8,600 acres of additional water were acquired. Some of the various types of facilities that were completed or under construction, at Ohio's thirty-five state parks, twenty-two state forests, and eighty-five wild life areas were:

> *324 family vacation lodge room units.*
> *215 year around family vacation cabins.*
> *3,416 class A campsites.*
> *2-1/4 miles of new public bathing beaches.*
> *Docking facilities for over 5,000 boats.*
> *325 miles of interior access highways.*
> *Parking areas for 48,000 vehicles.*
> *61 boat launching ramps.*
> *10 marine complexes.*
> *Four golf courses.*
> *40 projects to improve fishing in Ohio.*
> *Thousands of new picnic tables and grills.*
> *Hundreds of miles of hiking and horseback riding trails.*

The sixteen years of the Rhodes' administrations were marked by great strides in managing and conserving the state's natural resources, creating jobs, and opening outdoor recreation opportunities to millions of people.

The state park system became one of the best in the nation and Ohio's scenic rivers and natural area programs became models for the rest of the country. Progress was considerable in increasing the state's water and forest resources. The Clean Up Ohio Program to combat the state's litter problem gained national attention. Thanks to wise management, Ohio can boast again of an abundance of many game species.

Every resident in Ohio is touched in some way by a program of the Ohio Department of Natural Resources. The drink of clean water from the kitchen faucet, the walk through the woods at a park, the natural gas furnace that heats your home in winter, the coal burned to generate electricity, the wood used to build a livestock pen—these are functions we take for granted, functions in which the Department of Natural Resources (ODNR) played an important role.

The record of the Rhodes' years include:

|  | 1962 | 1982 |
|---|---|---|
| Number of state parks | 49 | 71 |
| Number of lodges/rooms | 1/32 | 7/589 |
| Number of cabins | 124 | 539 |
| Number of campsites | 2,100 | 9,285 |
| Number of marinas | 1 | 16 |
| Number of golf courses | 0 | 5 |
| Total ODNR acres | 303,082 | 380,243 |
| ODNR budget | $14,159,291 | $54,596,308 |

## Division of Civilian Conservation

The Civilian Conservation Corps organized and operated during the Rhodes' years proved to be a major asset to conservation in Ohio while developing one of our most precious resources—the youth of Ohio. About

5,000 Ohioans ages 16–23 participated in the Division of Civilian Conservation programs during the second eight years of his administrations. In addition, ODNR employed approximately 10,000 youths ages 15–18 in the Youth Conservation Corps.

YCC crews completed projects valued at more than $13 million. Those projects included flood control measures, construction of park trails, mapping parkland, restoring historical structures, timber cutting, reforestation, park improvement, and forest fire suppression and disaster services.

**Division of Forestry**

The proof of forestry progress lies in Ohio's forestland. During the Rhodes administrations, Ohio's forest acreage grew from 5.4 to 6.9 million acres.

Likewise, the saw-timber volume increased forty-two percent, from 14,374 million board feet to 20,416 board feet. While this was occurring, over 300 million board feet were harvested annually. Even more significant, growing stock volume grew by sixty-four percent. Another accomplishment is the enlargement and improvement of Ohio's nineteen state forests. Over 6,800 acres of land were added to the state forest system at a cost of $1.1 million. The state forests became more accessible and enjoyable for many recreational activities. For example, about a hundred miles of forest roads were paved or sealed to provide smooth, dust free surfaces for motorists, and over 238 miles of horse trails were laid out and five horseman camps established.

## Division of Natural Areas

The Department of Natural Resources made great progress in protecting many of the state's natural wonders during the Rhodes' administrations. In 1968, Ohio passed the nation's first scenic-river law, which became a model for subsequent federal legislation on scenic waterways. In 1970, Rhodes penned the Ohio Natural Areas Bill authorizing ODNR to purchase and administer state natural preserves and to protect privately owned natural areas. The Division of Natural Areas and Preserves was created in 1975, during Rhodes' third term of office.

## Division of Oil and Gas

The Division of Oil and Gas, created by the passage of House Bill 234 during the 106th General Assembly, became a division of the Department of Natural Resources on October 15, 1965. From a total of 12,918,000 barrels in 1965, Ohio's annual oil production, after falling to a sixteen-year low of 8,796,000 barrels in 1973, grew to a total of 13,551,000 barrels in 1981. Oil reserves grew from 101,024,000 barrels in 1965 to an estimated 144,003,000 in 1981. Natural gas production and reserves both showed a steady increase. The total volume of natural gas produced in Ohio during 1981 reached a total of 1,689 billion cubic feet.

## Division of Parks and Recreation

In response to Rhodes' call for a "system of state parks second to none," the Division of Parks and Recreation for twenty years placed a high priority on achieving this goal.

Emphasis was focused on purchasing new recreation land, improving existing facilities, and adding public oriented programs on outdoor education and recreation. Year-round attendance figures steadily increased during Rhodes' terms in office. The attendance figures reached a peak of fifty-two million visitors in 1981.

## Division of Reclamation

Ohio is coal country and the mining of the "black gold" was one of the state's most vital industries during the Rhodes years. Underground mining reached its peak in the early 1900s, but the advent of modern technology in the 1940s saw the rise of strip mining as the predominant method of coal extraction. In the early 1970s, Ohio's first comprehensive strip-mining law was passed and the division of reclamation came into being within ODNR. The general assembly passed the Industrial Minerals Law in 1975, giving the division regulatory authority in the extraction of sand, gravel, limestone, peat, and incidental coal.

## Division of Soil and Water Conservation

Between 1962 and 1982, ODNR mapped and classified 14.1 million acres of land, completed soil surveys of forty-one counties, published thirty-three county soil survey reports, and conducted 8,000 soil evaluations for property owners. The division administered Ohio's eighty-eight county soil and water conservation districts (SWCDs) that provided technical assistance in developing management plans yearly for some 100,000 private and public landowners in rural and urban Ohio. The operating budgets of all SWCDs increased from $310,000 in 1962 to $3 million in 1982.

## Division of Water

The division of water became one of the nation's leading water management agencies during the Rhodes administrations. The division was the first in the United States to complete and publish a detailed inventory of water resources and uses. This led to completion of the much-heralded Ohio Water Plan that presented the specific project and costs to resolve water problems in each community. Between 1962 and 1982, eleven major public water supply reservoirs were built in cooperation with user cities. Other construction projects undertaken included sixteen major flood control structures, modernization of the Ohio River lock and dam system, restoration of the Muskingum lock and dam system, a regional water system at Burr Oak, plus the planning of six multipurpose U.S. Army Corps of Engineers reservoirs. Many projects were completed with the assistance of the corps of engineers.

## Division of Watercraft

As participation in recreational boating in Ohio increased, so did the need for enforcement on the water, as well as the education of the boating public. The marine patrol assistance program, initiated in 1963, provided funding up to $10,000 each year to encourage local subdivisions to place greater emphasis on safe boating. During the Rhodes administration, twenty communities participated in the program.

## Division of Wildlife

In 1962, there were fewer than 35,000 white-tailed deer in Ohio and almost no bald eagles or wild turkeys. Fishing off the Ohio shore of Lake Erie was virtually non-existent. All of this changed during the Rhodes' years. The state's deer population increased dramatically over the two decades. An increased deer harvest, from 2,074 in 1963 to 47,634 in 1981, and the greater number of hunters, from 33,000 in 1963 to more than 230,000 in 1981, was the result. Deer hunters spent about $16 million a year in pursuit of game. Ohio's wild turkey population grew from experimental transplants in the early 1960s to populations that existed in thirty-two counties with over 2,900 square miles of range. About 5,000 to 8,000 turkeys roamed Ohio's woodlands at that time. During the sixteen years of the Rhodes administration, the division of wildlife distributed to conservation organizations over 785,000 pheasants and thousands of quail.

The program of recreation and conservation during the Rhodes' years had twenty objectives. Since this contribution of the Rhodes' administration is so little understood, those objectives are listed here:

WATER DEVELOPMENT: Complete Ohio's water management plan to provide more reservoirs for water supply, flood control, and recreation, and to protect and properly use Ohio's stream and underground water system.

URBAN RIVER AND WATERFRONT DEVELOPMENT: Revitalize valuable downtown water resources for recreation, beauty and utility.

COASTAL ZONE MANAGEMENT: Improve and

protect Lake Erie and encourage proper development of adjacent land resources.

SOIL INVENTORY: Accelerate Ohio's soil survey to provide basic information for land use decision.

AGRICULTURE POLLUTION AND URBAN SEDIMENT CONTROL: Conserve scarce resources and prevent further pollution and sedimentation in streams and lakes.

REFOREST OHIO'S LANDS: Establish a priority to prevent wind erosion in northwest Ohio and to protect marginal agriculture and strip-mined areas.

WILDLIFE HABITAT IMPROVEMENT: Provide food and cover for wildlife; beautify the landscape.

LAND REBORN: Transform old scars and pollution sources in previously mined areas.

NON-GAME AND ENDANGERED SPECIES: provide professional management for all wildlife species, to improve wildlife diversity and human enjoyment of wildlife resources.

NATURAL HERITAGE: Seek out, classify, and protect unique natural scenic areas in Ohio.

ENERGY AND MINERAL RESOURCE ASSESSMENT: Intensify survey and analysis of Ohio's fossil fuels, aggregate, and other industrial minerals to protect Ohio's economic base.

PARK DEVELOPMENT: Expand state park facilities—four new lodges, 200 cabins, 1,600 campsites, four golf courses, six new beaches, and seven nature centers; purchase 16,000 acres of land.

SENIOR CITIZEN SERVICES: Provide special senior citizen facilities and programs on state parks, forests and wildlife areas and provide reduced user costs through the Golden Buckeye card.

FISH OHIO: Double fishing opportunities in Ohio in five years through cleaner waters, more stocking, and more fisherman access in Ohio waters.

REVISE BOAT LICENSE PROCEDURE: Simplify the registration of Ohio's 275,000 boats through the use of longer registration periods and registration by mail.

CLEAN-UP OHIO: Improve health and aesthetic values in Ohio by removing litter, recycling resources and beautifying communities.

OHIO YOUTH OPPORTUNITIES: Expand the Youth Conservation Corps program to include year-round activities that will provide youth education and job opportunities in productive work.

HUNTING OPPORTUNITIES: Increase hunting opportunities through expanded use of state-owned lands, and the encouragement of private landowners to open their land to public hunting.

COMMUNITY PARKS AND RECREATION: Intensify aid to local governments in the acquisition and development of community parks and recreation areas.

STATEWIDE TRAILS SYSTEM: Expand outdoor recreation opportunities by developing a network of hiking, biking and riding trails throughout Ohio.

### C. Making Ohio the Gateway to the West

During his successful campaign for governor in 1962, Rhodes sensed the people of the state were frustrated by delays in utilizing available funds to build needed roads. Poor roads were limiting the development of industry and making driving a problem for citizens. Travelers on Route 40 took two hours to get through Columbus. So the transportation system of the state received prompt attention. Rhodes hired Pearl Masheter as director of highways to give the leadership to the most massive road-building program ever initiated in the state.

The Ohio territory was called the nation's "Gateway to the West," due to the natural transportation endowments that allowed easy access to the western frontier. As Ohio grew into statehood, transportation began to grow beyond those "natural boundaries." Still, Ohio would have to continue to move forward in order to compete in the national marketplace. It would take progressive leadership and a dedication to expanding Ohio's transportation network to get the job done. Thus in 1963, when Rhodes first took office, Ohio's transportation needs became a major priority.

Opening the state to business and trade meant a committed effort by the state. A bond issue was passed by the voters in 1964 to push ahead Ohio's interstate program. Bond money was used to initiate plans and work on the proposed interstate system. Once federal interstate funds became available, the bond money was replaced and invested into another interstate section. Due to this policy, Ohio led the way in the development of the interstates. The leadership and fiscal responsibility of Governor Rhodes has never been equaled in city or state government. His problem always was keeping the electorate informed enough to keep up with his planning.

In 1968, a second bond issue was passed, placing money into the hands of county officials for improvements in the local area. This bond issue divided $500 million as follows: $250 million for the counties; $30 million for the transportation research center; $15 million for public access roads to state parks; and $204 million for state highways. For the first time, bond money would go to the local level and help upgrade many important routes. This progressive thinking in the development of Ohio's highway network was directly responsible for the growth in importance of Ohio to the nation. Rhodes did not want the highways to be limited by the past designs, therefore he sent Masheter to visit highway systems in other countries. Masheter was impressed with the "autobahns" in Germany and particularly the outer belts around cities. He brought this concept back to the governor and Rhodes became strongly supportive of such outer belts. The governor was always willing to learn from others, and a staff person could always disagree with him and make his point.

*D*uring the early Rhodes' years, a commitment was made to improve highways and transportation routes in southern Ohio through the Applachian Highway program. This program helped to open up the less industrialized areas of the state to new business and jobs for the residents. The growth of jobs also was promoted through the vocational and technical education programs. Once completed, the Appalachian Highway linked southern Ohio to travel and trade west and east. Throughout his long career as a prime mover of Ohio's needs, Rhodes always equated a strong and varied transportation system with a productive state economy.

Rhodes said that if it were possible, he would have a bridge across the Ohio River wherever there was a community. He said, "bridges provide access not only to Ohioans to travel to other states, but the reverse as well." The connections with the total interstate system placed

Ohio closer to more people and places than any other state. Within 600 miles resides two-thirds of American's population and nearly seventy percent of the nation's purchasing power.

Ohio's complex transportation system was not limited to the highway. During the early years of the first Rhodes' administration, the importance of providing safer airport runway facilities came to light. With the 1964 bond issue, $4 million was set for building 3,400-foot runways with lights, adequate to handle industrial air traffic. This money was divided among forty airports, each getting $100,000 to do upgrading. In 1966, the plan had been so successful, an additional $1.2 million was appropriated to finish twelve more airports. By the end of the first Rhodes administration there were eighty-four counties with airports capable of handling industrial aircraft, thus opening Ohio to expanding business opportunities.

In 1967, at the beginning of the second Rhodes' administration, the new bond issue then provided another $4 million. This time, each of the airports was given $50,000 to provide additional services such as terminal buildings, navigational equipment, or other kinds of improvements.

During both of the early Rhodes' administrations, the commitment was made to provide the state with modern airport facilities throughout all of the counties. Starting in 1972 there was to be no money for county installations until Governor Rhodes took office again.

After he was elected for the fourth term, $1.2 million was appropriated for the 1980–81 biennium. This money provided maintenance money to protect the investment already put into the county airport system. Twenty-two of the original runways built with the 1964 bond money were to be repaved. Due to this program, an airplane flying over the state is always within twenty miles of a paved and lighted runway.

*I*t was the goal of the Rhodes' administrations to interlock the various modes of transportation, forming a comprehensive transportation pattern. The moving of people within a city was as important as moving traffic between cities. Through offices in the Ohio Department of Transportation, small communities were helped to investigate their needs. The base was set during the Rhodes' years to meet the needs of the community, and for the additional changes that must come.

Ohio was the first state to qualify for and expend all of the federal funds made available for highway construction. The transportation system assisted in the development of jobs and easy access to all areas of the state.

Highway, air and public transportation all were elements that made up Ohio's transportation system. Ohio's extensive water system also was important in such a system. With two-thirds of Ohio's land mass bordered by two of the world's largest inland water systems, Rhodes coined the phrase, "Ohio: America's Fourth Seacoast." Ohio's eight deep water ports, two with a foreign trade zone, operated with the other modes of transportation, connecting Ohio goods and people with not only the nation but also the world.

The Rhodes' investments in highway construction are best understood from the record of federal receipts and disbursements during the years. That record is as follows:

| FISCAL YEAR | RECEIVED JULY 1 TO JUNE 30 | DISBURSED JULY 1 TO JUNE 30 |
|---|---|---|
| 1963 | $337,879,434 | $380,529,402 |
| 1964 | 384,818,268 | 389,281,203 |
| 1965 | 400,576,995 | 393,611,428 |
| 1966 | 509,369,302 | 452,024,913 |
| 1967 | 466,093,773 | 464,533,517 |
| 1968 | 457,179,303 | 481,271,263 |
| 1969 | 570,771,430 | 523,360,334 |
| 1970 | 538,246,354 | 525,506,187 |
| 1971 | 484,610,187 | 492,850,819 |
| 1972 | 487,102,139 | 483,842,270 |
| 1973 | 465,288,617 | 448.081,336 |
| 1974 | 417,686,430 | 479,472,848 |
| 1975 | 554,724,352 | 491,724,687 |
| 1976 | 564,544,522 | 510,002,811 |
| 1977 | 428,024,257 | 473,883,786 |
| 1978 | 462,694,238 | 514,261,007 |
| 1979 | 617,294,580 | 583,311,891 |
| 1980 | 621,951,676 | 606,641,172 |
| 1981 | 606,703,585 | 550,832,691 |

Rhodes knew what Ohio needed and moved boldly ahead to make effective use of the extensive federal funds available. He had the plans ready for construction, using state funds, so that as soon as the federal funds were available contracts could be let. The state funds replaced by the federal funds were then used to plan additional highway construction. Pearl Masheter knew highway construction, and he and the governor made quite a team.

## D. Professionalizing the Highway Patrol

The construction discussed in the preceding chapter also had an effect on the highway patrol. First and foremost was the construction of the training academy. It was placed on the grounds of the Ohio State Fair in Columbus. It not only served as the training facility for all troopers, but it also provided various forms of training for other law enforcement officers. Such officers came not only from Ohio, but thoughout the United States and some foreign countries. Construction of this facility was commenced January 1, 1964, and completed with dedication ceremonies on September 2, 1965.

Other patrol posts built and construction dates were as follows:

| Post | Started | Completed |
|------|---------|-----------|
| Mansfield | 7-2-64 | 12-3-65 |
| Medina | 7-28-64 | 12-22-65 |
| Sandusky | 10-23-64 | 9-11-66 |
| Eaton | 12-29-65 | 5-67 |
| Lebanon | 4-21-66 | 6-20-67 |
| Marietta | 3-11-67 | 4-01-68 |
| Zzanesville | 2-20-68 | 1-16-70 |
| Circleville | 6-24-68 | 4-30-69 |
| Zenia | 4-17-69 | 3-23-70 |

In addition, construction was started on patrol posts at Granville, Ohio (4-10-70) and Chardon, Ohio (9-24-70) during the second term in office but was completed during Governor Gilligan's term.

## E. Serving the senior citizens

Ohio's first program for its older citizens came into existence in 1965 when Governor Rhodes established the Ohio Administration of Aging as a separate division within the department of mental health and correction. He enlisted Martin Janis to head the new division and Janis gave it excellent leadership. Its first accomplishment was the development of Ohio's Golden Age Village. These were pioneering ventures that gained national attention as models for low-income housing for older persons.

The Ohio General Assembly, on November 23,1973, created the commission on aging, with twelve members appointed by the governor to three-year terms. The majority of the members were required to be over the age of 60 (this was during the Gilligan administration). In 1975, upon his return to office, Rhodes said that one of his important goals in the operation of the commission was to destroy the stereotyped image of an older person. The goal was not only to destroy the image as seen by others, but how older persons viewed themselves. To bring this about, the governor approved the development of a series of special events. That the goal was achieved was attested to by the recognition that Ohio's program received nationally and the long-term impact on Ohio's senior citizens.

Among these were:

The annual Governor's Conference on Aging, started in 1967, was the first statewide special event. It provided a platform for exchanging ideas and philosophies and was an outlet for older Ohioans to make their views known.

Senior Citizens Day was initiated in 1977 to honor older Ohioans. Honoring the governor's recommendation, the legislature established the third Tuesday of May as Senior Citizens Day in Ohio. Over 250,000 persons took part annually in statewide senior citizen recognition activities in all of Ohio's eighty-eight counties.

Over 100,000 senior citizens participated regularly in physical fitness programs held at senior citizen centers and other places. To emphasize the importance of walking, an annual day was set aside for an Elderwalk program. In every community of the state, on the date established, senior citizens walked two miles. The program developed to where more than 100,000 persons participated in this annual event.

The Governor's Art Show, Sale, and Auction was held in the rotunda of the state capitol, a showcase for artistic talents of those aged 60 and older. It was established in 1976 and in several years had 7,844 entries, with a total sale of approximately $100,000, all of which went to the senior citizen artists.

In 1976, the first handmade Christmas ornaments by senior citizens decorated the official senior citizen's Christmas tree on the grounds of the state capitol. Each year a centenarian assisted the governor in an official lighting ceremony.

In 1978, Ohio's Senior Hall of Fame was established to recognize contributions made by Ohioans over the age of 60, and to promote the fact that age has nothing to do with continuing contributions. A total of seventy-three persons were inducted into the hall of fame between 1978 and September 13, 1991, the 80th birthday of Governor Rhodes.

On the basis of the strong commitment of the governor to physical fitness, a program was begun in 1978 to emphasize the importance of physical exercise.

Over 100,000 senior citizens participated regularly in physical fitness programs held in senior citizens centers and other places.

One of the most innovative and successful programs ever developed in a governmental agency was conceived and implemented by Rhodes in 1976 with the birth of the Golden Buckeye Card. Over 1.2 million older Ohioans carry the Golden Buckeye Card, which is honored by over 31,000 merchants.

*U*nder Rhodes, the legislature established Ohio's energy credit program, funded totally by the state to provide assistance with paying winter heating bills. This program began in 1978, and was funded at an approximate cost of $40 million annually.

Ohio has been given national recognition for the development of senior citizen centers and multipurpose centers. Legislation adopted in 1979 gave authority to the Ohio Commission on Aging to spearhead the development and expansion of such centers. Since then over $20 million in new, expanded, or remodeled construction has been initiated on a cooperative basis with individual local communities. This partnership between the local communities of Ohio and the state has resulted in the development of more than 414 senior citizen centers and multipurpose centers serving as focal points for the activities of senior citizens within their respective communities.

Ohio was selected by two different groups to receive awards of grants for the development of long-term care alternatives to nursing home care. One of the grants was from the department of health and human services and the other from the Robert Wood Johnson Foundation.

In addition to funding providers of services to older persons since 1965, Ohio developed an extensive nutritious meal program. In 1976, Ohio completed the goal of establishing at least one nutrition site in each of the eighty-eight counties. There were 250 locations serving 15,000 meals daily at that time. Since, 188 new sites were added so that in 1991 a total of 26,000 meals were served daily.

# The family

*"When everything else is gone, what you have left is family."*
—James A. Rhodes

James A. Rhodes has been heralded, arguably true, as the "governor of the century" but his continuing interest and the basis for his strength in office was always his family. In retirement, his family continued to be his reason for living and the basis of his continuing happiness and strength. During the sixteen years that he served as governor, little was published about his family and Mrs. Rhodes did not participate actively in public life. Never, however, did the governor forget the basis of his strength or abandon the family for the fanfare of office. The measure of his devotion to his family is an untold story.

208

James A. Rhodes and family, 1962: daughter Sherrie at left; Helen; and daughters Sue and Saundra.

James A. Rhodes and Helen Rawlins were married in 1941, after he had been elected as auditor of Ohio in 1940. Helen was a beautiful girl and James A.'s one love for life. Helen was not one to share a man with any other woman and let James A. know right from the beginning there was to be no other woman in his life. They had forty-five years of married life and James A. always expressed his love for her.

Their first home was a rented apartment and the future governor was serving as the state auditor. Money was not plentiful but adequate for their needs. Their main recreation was playing bridge with Richard and Lucy

Davis on the weekends. Helen Rhodes never really cared for the public life but as the wife of a person elected to office she knew that politics was James A.'s future, and she went along with the decision.

Susan Sybil Rhodes was born while they lived at the apartment and the living quarters became tight with the new child and Grandmother Rhodes. The family looked at a home on Nottingham Road in North Columbus. The real estate agent was John Jacobs Sr. and Mrs. Rhodes and Mother Rhodes decided the house was what they wanted. James A. didn't have much choice in the matter, except the worry of how to pay off the great amount—for that day—of $6,500. Susan, his daughter, remembers the place as a wonderful home with a lot of space and a tennis court behind.

$\mathcal{T}$ he family grew to three girls and the three girls and their families became the great pride and joy of the governor. The girls and their families are as follows:

Susan Sybil was born in 1942 and married Richard H. Moore in 1963. Their children are Melissa ("Missy"), born 1964; Richard H., Jr., born 1966; James Rhodes, 1967; Jason, 1971; and Allyson Lynn, 1973.

Saundra Ann was born in 1945 and married Dr. John Jacob Jr., a dentist. Their children are Sharon Sue (adopted), born 1971, and James John (Jimmy John), 1972. Saundra died March 22, 1996.

Sharon Lou was born in 1950 and married William Markham, Florida. Their children are James Rhodes, born 1980, and William Robert, born 1985.

The children report that mother was the disciplinarian.

Dinner was at 5:30 p.m., and the girls— and father—were expected to be there. Most often, father had to go back out for meetings in the evening. Father might run the city or later the state, but mother ran the house and the family.

Susan remembered that when her father had several days free, he would come home and on the spur of the moment say, "Pack up the girls and let's go." Off they would go to some resort. Every winter they arranged to go to Pokagon State Park in Indiana for skiing. James A. did not ski but arranged for the girls to enjoy the experience.

Normally after an election, there would be a week trip to somewhere as a means of relaxation. They often vacationed with Lee, Helen's sister, and Jim Reardon and their three boys. The three boy cousins were about the same age as the Rhodes' three girls. It seemed that every place they vacationed, there was a golf course. The governor loved golf and no vacation was complete unless he had an opportunity to play. He was good at the game and played many times with famous people.

For many years, he played as an amateur in the Bob Hope Classic. He was a long time member of the Scioto Country Club where he started the golf tournaments for caddies. He played golf with Mr. Honda when he visited Ohio and the Honda Plant was under construction, and his last home backed up to the Scioto Country Club golf course.

Susan remembered the whole family going to county and state fairs long before James A. became governor and made the Ohio State Fair the largest in the nation.

She and her son, Rick, remember visiting all of the county fairs one summer when her father was governor. Rick remembered that they visited eight to ten fairs a day. At times when he was governor, places he visited planned banquets for him but he usually thanked them kindly and lived on hot dogs and pop. He seldom took the time to relax over a dinner.

While the family lived on Nottingham Road there were always many children around the house. The tennis court was for use by all of the boys and girls in the neighborhood. Helen and James A. played tennis together at home and she played golf with him as the children were growing up. As they moved to Scenic Drive, off Weisheimer Road, James A. built a lighted basketball court behind the house and it became the gathering spot for all of the boys in the neighborhood. James A. played with them when time permitted.

There was a creek behind the house and he would take the girls—and any other children handy—down to the creek to fish. He provided the fishing poles. When he became mayor of Columbus, his girls and many other children liked to ice skate behind The Ohio State University on the Olentangy River, but it was a dark area. Mayor Rhodes had the recreation department set up lights for the skaters and took hot dogs and hot chocolate down to them.

During his band-booking days, James A. became acquainted with many celebrities in the entertainment field. When they came into town he had them out to his house. The girls were entranced and their friends were welcome to visit the celebrities. Susan recalls when Pat Boone visited their home while she was in high school, Rhodes invited a hundred of her friends to meet him. Whenever Hopalong Cassidy or Gene Autry was in town they visited the Rhodes home. Roy Rogers was an annual visitor. Each of the three Rhodes girls was permitted to have a ride on Trigger, Roy Rogers's famous horse.

Rhodes loved his children as well as his work in public office. Each of the three girls had a horse and was trained to ride. They participated in horse shows and they could count on their father to attend such events. The horses were kept at the Duros stables initially and later at the River Ridge Riding Academy. When the snow was on the ground in Columbus, James A. would take the girls to Whetstone Park in the north part of Columbus for sledding. The girls would sled down the hill, and then he would pull six or seven sleds back up the hill with the car.

*J*ames A. liked a lot of people around. When the family went on a trip, he encouraged them to take along one or two friends. Helen Rhodes never knew how many there would be for dinner. James A. might just walk in with two or three friends or staff members for dinner. Rhodes especially liked young people and children. Never a great disciplinarian, his grandchildren had the run of the house when they visited him. At least once a week, the members of the family who lived in the vicinity of Columbus, gathered for a Sunday meal.

Just before Susan graduated from high school, James A. and Helen invited the entire senior class to breakfast at their home. There were five hundred students in the class and about three hundred of them came. The three girls loved White Castle hamburgers. While he was mayor he would go to the White Castle restaurant on High Street at the foot of Arcadia Avenue and get ten or twelve dozen burgers for the children and their friends.

When the grandchildren came along and entered

school, James A. was governor. He would invite the grandchildren and their classmates to visit the statehouse. After a tour, he served them Wendy's sandwiches in the cabinet room.

Rick, Jamie, and Jason, children of Susan and Richard H. Moore, played basketball for Upper Arlington High School and James A. never missed a game. Each of the three boys was elected team captain. He also followed the efforts of Jimmy John, son of Saundra and Dr. John Jacob Jr., as he served as captain of the golf team. The activities of his grandchildren were the only things that caused him to miss a meeting. Rick and Jamie played together after high school at a junior college in Florida, and Rick played basketball at Otterbein College in Westerville.

Mrs. Rhodes didn't travel often with the governor in his latter years in office, but she did travel with him while he was mayor of Columbus. She even went with him to visit some of the foreign offices that he established. The girls recall they often went with James A. and their mother to conferences and meetings.

The 4th of July celebration was a big day for the family. James A. would purchase a large quantity of fireworks and in the evening they went to the home of Jerry Kaltenbach in Hilliard, and had two hours of bangs and colorful explosions. Jerry was a long-term friend of the governor's and served as fair manager when the state fair became the largest in the nation.

When James A. decided to run for a third term as governor, Helen Rhodes made one demand. If he were elected, they would continue to live in their house in Upper Arlington. James A. agreed, and during his third and fourth terms as governor, they continued to live at their home on Tremont Road.

Susan said that her father did not send the children to Sunday school and church; he went with them. James A.'s mother was a staunch Methodist, but he became a Presbyterian when the group of young men wanted to play ball on the Presbyterian ground in Jackson, Ohio.

He and the family belonged to the Overbrook Presbyterian Church while they lived in Columbus, and the girls were married there. When he moved to Upper Arlington, his grandchildren attended Upper Arlington Lutheran Church, so he began attending there.

The forty-five year love story came to a close in 1987. Helen Rhodes became seriously ill while James A. was running for a fifth term as governor. The campaign was going badly because his supporters did not provide the money needed for television and radio programs. Mrs. Rhodes was hospitalized in Cleveland during the campaign and James A. immediately suspended his campaigning and went to her side. He remained there until she could return to their home in Columbus. A reporter told about seeing him slumped over in sleep at her bedside.

Helen Rhodes had the arteries replaced in her legs during her stay in the Cleveland Clinic. The family placed a hospital bed downstairs after her return from the clinic and James A. slept on the couch near her. She would not have any outside nursing help in and the family took turns assisting her. She lived approximately a year after leaving the Cleveland Clinic.

Susan, her daughter, remembered that she left the house to go to the grocery and was called home from there. The squad was called but Mrs. Rhodes died on

December 9, 1987, a week before her and the governor's forty-sixth wedding anniversary.

The death of Helen Rhodes caused a separation of the two of them but not an end of his love and the love of the family for this strong lady with a great sense of humor.

At ninety, Rhodes knew the wisdom of the statement reported at the beginning of this chapter, "When all else is gone, what you have left is family." He was still in demand for advising persons in public life and for presentations and honors from persons and organizations that recognized him as "The Governor of the Century." His greatest joy and the basis of his happiness, however, was his loving and supportive family. Far beyond any money and fame, he was always wealthy in family and friends.

# The afterglow

When James A. Rhodes left the governor's office in 1982, he had been a campaigner eighteen times in a fifty-four year political career. He had lost three times and was destined to lose once more. With the fourth loss his winning average was seventy-five percent. His record is not likely to be ever repeated again. In his administrations as governor, the state was rebuilt for education, industry, recreation, and transportation. All the while, urban populations and population as a whole, grew dramatically and then leveled nearly to a stop.

His campaigns are reported herein as summarized by T. H. Dudgeon in previous writings:

Rhodes with wife,
Helen, circa 1985.

| Number | Year | JAR's Age | Office | Result |
|--------|------|-----------|--------------|--------|
| 1 | 1934 | 25 | Committeeman | Won |
| 2 | 1936 | 27 | Committeeman | Won |
| 3 | 1938 | 29 | Schoolboard | Won |
| 4 | 1939 | 30 | City Auditor | Won |
| 5 | 1941 | 32 | City Auditor | Won |
| 6 | 1943 | 33 | Mayor | Won |
| 7 | 1947 | 37 | Mayor | Won |

| Number | Year | JAR's Age | Office | Result |
|--------|------|-----------|--------|--------|
| 8 | 1950 | 40 | Governor (Primary) | Lost |
| 9 | 1951 | 41 | Mayor | Won |
| 10 | 1952 | 42 | State Auditor | Won |
| 11 | 1954 | 44 | Governor | Lost |
| 12 | 1956 | 46 | State Auditor | Won |
| 13 | 1960 | 50 | State Auditor | Won |
| 14 | 1962 | 52 | Governor | Won |
| 15 | 1966 | 56 | Governor | Won |
| 16 | 1970 | 60 | US Senate (Primary) | Lost |
| 17 | 1974 | 64 | Governor | Won |
| 18 | 1978 | 68 | Governor | Won |
| 19 | 1986 | 76 | Governor | Lost |

When James A. left the office of governor in 1982, he was financially independent. He not only had a pension from his years in public office, he had amassed wealth from his business activities in the four years he was out of office between 1970 and 1974. He immediately went back into business as a consultant to people in industry and commerce who wanted to sell their products overseas. He set up an office at 44 East Gay Street and started work the day after he left the governor's office. He didn't need the money, but he could not retire to a sedentary life. People and their challenges had been his goal in government, and retiring was not an option.

The day after the 1986 loss to Celeste, Rhodes was back in his office working as a consultant to industry and business. He never had time to bemoan the past or argue why he didn't win. It was on to the future.

During a visit to a basketball game at the Silverdome stadium in Detroit, one of his grandchildren with him asked, "Why don't they put houses in a circle and build a dome over the inside area so people can play even when it's raining or snowing?"

Rhodes went back to the office with an idea that fitted in with an invention on which he had been working, with the help of the Lennox Heating and Air-conditioning Company—a filtration system that would remove over ninety-nine percent of the germs and bacteria from the air in a house.

He made a model of a housing development designed in a circle, with the center area covered by a dome that would include the new filtered air system. Over a period of years, he worked hard to sell the idea to developers but none would invest in the concept. He then adapted the "germ and bacteria free" filtration system to individual homes and installed the system in his home on Tremont Road and in a home built outside Los Angeles. The system in his home was reviewed and praised by the American Lung Association and such a system was later installed in its national offices.

The year James A. became 80, Vernal G. Riffe, speaker of the house of representatives in Ohio, and Stanley J. Aronoff, the president of the Ohio Senate, honored him at a big birthday party. The party was held at the Aladdin Mosque and attended by nearly a thousand people, happy to help him celebrate his 80th birthday. The recognition was bipartisan, since Verne Riffe was a highly recognized Democrat and Stanley Aronoff a leading Republican. James A. Rhodes' recognition for his contributions to Ohio and his ability to work with the opposite party went beyond party politics.

A book entitled *James A. Rhodes at Eighty,* describing his last campaign for public office, was commissioned by Riffe and Aronoff and published as a group birthday greeting by his friends. Copies of the book were made available free of charge to his friends attending the birthday party on September 13, 1989.

On the occasion of his 82nd birthday, Riffe and Aronoff again hosted a birthday party and honored James A. as "Ohio's Governor of the Century." They published a book extolling his leadership and programs entitled, *Ohio's Governor of the Century, James A. Rhodes, Ohio Governor 1963–1971 and 1975–1983.* The book was written by Tom Dudgeon, who has since passed away.

*J*ames A. continued his work as a consultant at his office at 44 East Gay Street and continued to promote the installation of his clean air system for hospitals and homes. At one point he proposed to purchase about forty-three acres of land in Upper Arlington in order to build homes and condominiums that included the new system. He was not permitted to purchase the land for construction as he proposed since the city fathers wanted that parcel to be used for a purpose that would bring more taxes to the city.

In 1996, he moved his office to a building near Tremont and Henderson Roads. By that time, James Duerck had retired and only Pauline Yee was left from his original staff. Two of his grandsons joined him in the office and assisted him with the consulting for industry and business and promotion of the "germ free air system."

About this time, James A. fell and broke his hip, which triggered other medical problems. The broken hip and other illnesses slowed his ability to get around but did not limit his drive and spirit. In 1997, he closed his office and worked out of his home with the assistance of "Rick" Moore, his grandson. The other grandson who was with him opened a business of his own.

Each year for the last six years of the governor's life, Phillip Hamilton organized a birthday dinner for the governor at Der Dutchman Restaurant in Plain City. Colleagues from all of his administrations turned out. The last such dinner was September 13, 1998. The governor attended and the party room at the restaurant was packed. Seventeen years after he left office, the people with whom he had worked came together to celebrate the "Camelot years" and to honor their leader. Even after his death, several dinners were organized for former staff and friends by Phil Hamilton at the governor's beloved restaurant, the most recent on the governor's birthday in September of 2004.

As James A. Rhodes celebrated his 90th birthday, he planned to live to be a hundred years old and embarked on planning a new venture in home construction. The partners had plans to build 380 living units, including both individual houses and condominiums. The "clean air and germ free system" developed by Rhodes was to be offered as an option in the homes.

On April 24, 1999, James A. was honored by being chosen as the honoree for the Scottish Rite Reunion, to raise Master Masons to the 32nd degree, and the Aladdin Temple Shrine Ceremonial to make such Masons members of the Shrine. He had been a DeMolay when he was a young man, which is a Masonic organization for youths 12 to 21 years of age. He joined the Neoacacia Masonic Lodge #595 in Columbus in 1951 and was raised to the Master Masonic degree that year. In 1981, he was awarded the Scottish Rite 33rd degree in Washington, DC. This is the highest honor that can be achieved in the Masonic order and is awarded to only a few people, on the basis of their service to the public or the Masonic organization. James A. received the award in his fourth term as governor, on the basis of his service to the people of Ohio.

On the same April 24, 1999, at an evening dinner meeting, James A. was presented the Fourth Annual Golden Arm award by the Upper Arlington Chamber of Commerce. The award is given to one person a year for citizenship and human services.

James A. made presentations at each of the meetings.

*I*n March of 1999, he sold his large house on Tremont Road and moved into an apartment in the Forum Retirement Center on Henderson Road, near Kenny Road. His movements were hampered by his injuries but he got around as needed. He followed the admonition he gave to a staff member when he was governor: "Don't look back, something might be gaining on you."

He died on March 4, 2001, at Riverside Methodist Hospital, in Columbus. He had contracted pneumonia and was in the hospital for several days but returned home before going into the hospital for the last time.

It was my privilege to meet with him on the day before he returned to the hospital for the last time. The last thing he said to me was, "When you come back, we will arrange to publish the biography."

The funeral for the governor was a recognition worthy of the great man. He laid in state at the Upper Arlington Lutheran Church at Mill Run on the first evening and the capitol building in Columbus, Ohio, on the second day. A recognition service was held in the capital building with presentations given by many of his friends and colleagues. Friends and co-workers from his administrations lined the route from the place of the service to the waiting funeral hearse.

The funeral service was held at the Upper Arlington Lutheran Church at Mill Run and a mile-long funeral procession wound its way to his final resting place in a mausoleum at Greenlawn Cemetery in Columbus.

To the end, James A. served the people of Ohio honestly and creatively, making massive improvements in all levels of education, transportation, natural resources, industrial and business development, opportunities for youth, public buildings, senior citizen activities, museums and cultural centers. He presided over a balanced budget for sixteen years.

When he left the governor's office for the first time in 1972, after thirty-six years in public office, his total fiscal worth was $65,000, including the value of his pension. In the four years before he ran successfully for governor again, he made himself enough money that he didn't need to worry about that problem again.

At 90, he still believed that "profit is not a dirty word" and was actively engaged in planning a construction project.

James A. Rhodes intended to live to be a hundred, and as long as he lived, he worked, and he was interested in the welfare of Ohio.

The only things that ever took preference over

his duties in office were the needs and interests of his family.

When James A. Rhodes met his maker, he could say, "I did my best and I cheated no man."

*There are thousands to tell you it cannot be done,*
*There are thousands who prophesy failure;*
*There are thousands to point out to you, one by one,*
*The dangers that await to assail you.*
*But just buckle in with a bit of a grin,*
*Just take off your coat and go to it;*
*Just start to sing as you tackle the thing*
*That "cannot be done" and you'll do it.*
                    —Edgar A. Guest

# THE AFTERGLOW
*Chapter sixteen*

# $\mathcal{I}ndex$

# About the author

Bryl R. Shoemaker, a Columbus, Ohio, native, began his long career in education by dropping out of The Ohio State University. After marriage and two children, he returned to the university, graduated with a major in education, and later achieved both the Master of Arts and Ph.D.

He taught in three different school systems, spent two years in the Navy as curriculum officer for one of the advanced technical schools in Washington, D.C., and for nearly a quarter of a century, he was Ohio's Director of Vocational and Career Education, where he worked intimately with Governor Rhodes to develop the state's system of vocational and career education, as well as the initiation of the first thirteen two-year post-high school technical institutes.

After retirement, Dr. Shoemaker worked thirteen more years with the National Institute for Automotive Service Excellence. There, he established the national system for evaluating and certifying automotive technician training programs that met the automotive industry's national standards.

He has been married to Dorothy Curren for 67 years. They have three children, seven grandchildren, thirteen great grandchildren, and three great great grandchildren.